Milk Substitutes - Selected Aspects

Edited by Małgorzata Ziarno

Published in London, United Kingdom

IntechOpen

Supporting open minds since 2005

Milk Substitutes - Selected Aspects
http://dx.doi.org/10.5772/intechopen.87527
Edited by Małgorzata Ziarno

Contributors
Jyotika Dhankhar, Preeti Kundu, Youssouf Toukourou, Abdoulaye Moubarack, Roselina Karim, Nor Aini Mat Noh, Shafa'Atu Giwa Ibrahim, Wan Zunairah Wan Ibadullah, Norhasnida Zawawi, Nazamid Saari, Małgorzata Ziarno, Anna Veber, Dorota Zaręba, Ewa Kowalska, Patrycja Cichońska, Suzana Caetano Da Silva Lannes, Laís Zandona, Caroline Lima

First published in London, United Kingdom, 2021 by IntechOpen
IntechOpen is the global imprint of INTECHOPEN LIMITED, registered in England and Wales, registration number: 11086078, 5 Princes Gate Court, London, SW7 2QJ, United Kingdom
Printed in Croatia

British Library Cataloguing-in-Publication Data
A catalogue record for this book is available from the British Library

Additional hard and PDF copies can be obtained from orders@intechopen.com

Milk Substitutes - Selected Aspects
Edited by Małgorzata Ziarno
p. cm.
Print ISBN 978-1-78985-637-8
Online ISBN 978-1-83880-768-9
eBook (PDF) ISBN 978-1-83880-769-6

Meet the editor

Małgorzata Ziarno is a professor at the Institute of Food Sciences, Warsaw University of Life Sciences (SGGW-WULS), Poland. Her professional interests include production systems and quality of dairy products and their plant substitutes, analysis and evaluation of dairy products and their plant substitutes, food production hygiene and food quality control, application of lactic acid bacteria and propionic acid bacteria in food production and bioprotection, production of functional food, and modifying the nutritional value. Privately, she is a person with a wide range of interests and a wealth of hobbies, including food, cultivation of plants, astronomy, and cosmonautics as well as music and computer games.

Contents

Preface

Foods based on milk, as well as those containing milk, are important elements in the human diet. Unfortunately, due to containing ingredients that may cause intolerance or allergy, these products cannot be consumed by consumers suffering from hypersensitivity to lactose, galactose, or milk proteins. People suffering from this dysfunction must often eliminate milk and dairy products from their diet. Similar exclusions are made by people opting for veganism or other forms of elimination diets with an ideological, ethical, or health background. The response to this tendency and consumer expectations is the creation of new brands of veg producers, as well as the introduction of plant variants to the offer of large companies. It is influenced by the increasing nutritional awareness of people, more affordable prices, and the increasing availability of ready-made vegan or vegetarian products. At the same time, the number of people who consume a traditional diet but willingly include plant dishes is increasing. This is explained by the desire to diversify the nutritional and taste profile of the diet. The increasing tendency of allergies to animal proteins, including milk proteins, as well as lactose intolerance, is not without significance for expanding the availability of plant substitutes. In connection with all of this, a serious challenge for the food industry is the development of new, alternative products with attractive tastes and comparable nutritional values to replace dairy products. More and more shops and restaurants are offering plant-based equivalents of animal products.

Factors such as increasing pro-health awareness, more frequent occurrence of allergies and lifestyle diseases, and an increasing number of vegan consumers have contributed to the growing demand for alternative products. The dairy product alternatives market began its development with dairy drinks as milk substitutes. The plant beverages market is growing both in terms of the scale of production and the variety of raw materials used in the production of beverages. Soybean was one of the first raw materials used to produce vegetable drinks in the form of milk substitutes. Its popularity within this product category is weakening in favor of others, such as nuts (almonds, hazelnuts, cashews, ground almonds), grains (oats, rice, quinoa, buckwheat, millet, corn, and kamut wheat, spelt) and hemp, sunflower or chia seeds as well as coconut or banana fruit. In addition, the raw materials that diversify and enrich plant-based drinks provide taste, color, and aroma. It is worth emphasizing that plant drinks are a source of fiber and other ingredients such as vitamins D, B12, and B2, which are enriched in these types of products and at the same time do not contain cholesterol and lactose. According to all forecasts, the Polish market for plant drinks will develop dynamically. Its development will be based on expanding the range of raw materials that meet gluten-free and high nutritional values, based on natural ingredients, and originating from organic farming. Currently, the most popular plant drinks are rice milk, which has a delicate taste, and oat milk, which has a mild taste and contains naturally occurring prebiotic substances like beta-glucan. Oat milk can also be made gluten-free. Beverages such as coconut, millet, and almond milk are extremely popular due to their characteristic organoleptic feature. It is probably only a matter of time before beverages from other previously unused sources appear on the market, for example, grains, nuts, or other plant parts. The greatest technological difficulty in the plant-based market is the stabilization of beverages. Stabilization of the fluid structure ensures uniform dispersion of particles that will be durable regardless of the application. In most cases, manufacturers do not declare stabilizing additives, and therefore the consumer considers possible delamination. Stabilized drinks are characterized by a smoother and more stable structure. In addition to plant-based drinks, the market also offers plant-based creams, cheeses, butter, and fermented beverages based mostly on prepared vegetable proteins as well as coconut fat or other vegetable fats.

The nutritional importance of protein is confirmed not only in the diet of humans but also of animals. Nutritional problems on a global scale will force us to look for new vegetable sources of protein for feed for farm animals, especially in developing countries.

The increase in health problems, as well as the increased awareness of sustainable development, direct the processing and fodder industries to wider use of proteins of plant origin. The food industry should perceive the market of vegetable proteins not as a competition, but rather as a source of innovation for its own products based on cow, goat, or sheep milk. This takes advantage of the popularity of plant-based proteins, especially as some studies show that one in three consumers prefer plant-based over animal proteins. In addition, many plant-based protein products are strongly associated with sustainability and rated as having a low carbon footprint.

Małgorzata Ziarno
Department of Food Technology and Assessment,
Institute of Food Sciences,
Warsaw University of Life Sciences SGGW-WULS,
Warsaw, Poland

Section 1

Human Health and Consumer Acceptance

Chapter 1

Plant-Based Milk Substitutes: Factors to Lead to Its Use and Benefits to Human Health

Laís Zandona, Caroline Lima and Suzana Lannes

Abstract

The consumption of vegetable milk has grown in recent years. Medical reasons are some reasons for the increase in the number of consumers of this type of drink. Lactose intolerance and allergy to cow's milk protein are the major factors that lead to this consumption in addition to the option for a healthier lifestyle, there are also consumers concerned with animal health and welfare who are adept at restrictive diets like vegetarianism and veganism. Vegetable extracts are water-soluble extracts from legumes, oilseeds, cereals, or pseudocereals that resemble bovine milk in appearance, are considered substitutes for cow's milk due to the similar chemical composition and can also be used as substitutes for direct use or in some animal milk-based preparations. In contrast, these substitutes have different sensory characteristics, stability, and nutritional composition of cow's milk. Plant extracts have health-beneficial compounds, phenolic compounds, unsaturated fatty acids, antioxidant activity and bioactive compounds such as phytosterols and isoflavones making plant-based milk substitutes an interesting choice.

Keywords: functional food, lactose intolerance, cow protein milk allergy, veganism, bioactive compounds

1. Introduction

The animal milk is already a highly consumed and appreciated by the human being for many centuries. Its consumption may exist from 8000 BC to 10,000 BC through the aurochs, ancestors of the actual cows, were domesticated and its milk used for consumption [1].

Milk is a highly valued and important food for the human diet. Since birth, this food can provide nutrients capable of transmitting not only energy but also bioactive components and immune cells that are responsible for anti-inflammatory, anti-infectious, and probiotic actions [2].

Since milk is a food that contains almost all the nutrients necessary for the maintenance of our body, it is still widely consumed, even in adulthood. Nowadays, use the term "milk" for the secreted fluid of the cow, and the secreted fluid of other animals is called "animal name + milk", for example, sheep's milk, goat milk and buffalo milk [3].

Milk consumption is very important, especially in underdeveloped countries, as it is an important source of energy, protein and fat, being one of the most important foods for consumption in malnourished children [4].

For several reasons, more consumers choose alternatives to plant-based milk. The most common reasons are allergies to milk protein, lactose intolerance or lifestyle choices, such as vegetarianism [5].

Because of this, currently an increase in research and development of plant-based milks and their derivatives, such as yogurts, ice cream and fermented beverages, has been carried out in order to bring more consumption options for individuals who cannot or do not wish to consume animal milk. Thus, the objective of this chapter is providing some information on types of milk substitutes and their functionality in food formulations and in human health.

2. Animal milk: processing and composition

As a natural food, milk has a rapid multiplication of different microbial groups. Therefore, both raw milk and dairy products, with the exception of some cheeses, must go through a thermal process, such as pasteurization, thermization or ultra-high temperature (UHT) so that pathogenic microorganisms are eliminated and so the milk is safe for consumption [6].

The UHT process for milk is a technique that uses a heat treatment with temperature between 135 and 150°C with pause times between 1 and 10 s. There are two types of heating for this processing: direct and indirect heating. In direct heating, the milk itself encounters a saturated steam. In indirect heating, an external heating medium will indirectly heat milk by conduction and convection through a barrier that acts as a heat exchanger. The indirect heating is the most used by industries [7].

As for milk pasteurization, the milk is heated to a specific temperature, keeping the milk at this temperature for a specific length and successively a rapid cooling step with a temperature below 7°C. The temperature and length of the pasteurization process will depend on which microbial or chemical effects are desirable. When submitting milk to the pasteurization process, one must think that the higher the temperature and the longer the process, the drastic decrease in the number of microorganisms will be possible, but there will also be a damage to the nutritional constituents of milk [8].

As for the thermization technique, a temperature of 63°C is used for 15 s, being milder than pasteurization; this process is used only to improve the quality of the milk, since there is no effective elimination of pathogenic microorganisms that may be present in the milk [8].

From whole milk, several by-products, such as cream, buttermilk, skimmed milk, and derived by-products, such as caseins and whey protein can be produced by the dairy industry. The processing of both whole milk and these by-products can be seen in **Figure 1** [9].

Milk is a complex biological fluid that contains fat, proteins, vitamins, minerals, enzymes and sugar in its composition. Mammalian animals show similarities regarding the nutritional composition of their milks however, the influence of genetic factors, nutritional factors and environmental conditions can alter the composition of milk, even in animals of the same species. **Table 1** presents a general composition of the milk of different mammals [11].

Milk plays a fundamental role in human nutrition and health, which is why the intake of this food is so important to be consumed by both children and adults. The milk consumed by humans comes mainly from the dairy cattle, but in some parts of the world, there is the consumption of milk from other animal species, for example, buffalo, goats, sheep, and camels. Cow's milk protein consists of approximately 80% casein (w/w) and 20% of whey protein (w/w) [13].

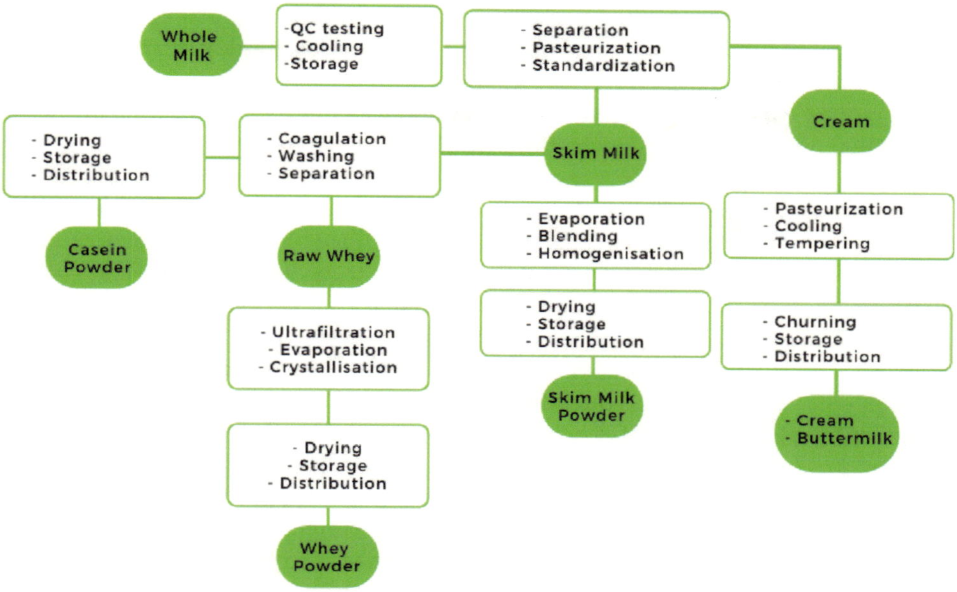

Figure 1.
Processing of whole milk and its by-products [10].

Species	Water	Proteins	Fat	Lactose	Ash
Cow	87.2	3.5	3.7	4.9	0.72
Sheep	82.7	5.5	6.4	4.7	0.92
Goat	86.5	3.6	4.0	5.1	0.82
Camel	87.7	3.5	3.4	4.7	0.71

Table 1.
The composition of milk from different mammals in g/100 g milk [12].

In animal milk, exist four main caseins that are naturally present: αs1, αs2, B e k, with casein k being the most relevant due to its importance in the stability of the micelle and in the processing of various dairy derivatives [12].

As for whey protein, the main proteins are β-lactoglobulin, α-lactalbumin, serum albumin, immunoglobulins (IgG1, IgG2, IgA and IgM) and lactoferrin. This class of proteins is classified as high biological value since it presents essential amino acids and branched chain amino acids (not synthesized by our organism). With this has received a lot of attention for the food development industry, mainly in sports nutrition, since that these amino acids are important for tissue growth and repair [14].

Bovine milk fat has more than 400 fatty acids with different chemical compositions. Its composition consists of triacylglycerol, diacylglycerol, free fatty acids, and cholesterol [15].

The composition of milk fat will in fact depend on external factors to which dairy cattle are subjected, such as factors related to food (feed offered to cattle) or rumen microbial activity. In addition, other factors such as stage of lactation and mastitis can also influence the final composition of milk fat [16].

Milk fat is the natural source that most presents short-chain fatty acids (C4:0 – C8:0) and also contains a high amount of medium chain fatty acids (C10:0 – C14:0) which causes that this food is almost exclusive to certain bioactive fatty acids considered beneficial to human health. An example of this is butyric acid (C4:0) and conjugated linoleic acid that are not found in significant amounts in other foods in our diet [17, 18].

Regarding carbohydrate, lactose is the main present in the composition of milk. This compound if formed by the union of a D-galactose molecule with a D-glucose molecule. Thus, lactose can be hydrolyzed through an enzymatic action by β-galactosidase that will transform it into its constituent monosaccharides, i.e., galactose and glucose. This action is of great importance for the food industry, since lactose, despite being a sugar, does not have a sweet taste, but its constituents have such a sweet taste, in addition to being more soluble than lactose [12, 19].

In addition, when lactic acid bacteria meet with lactose, they hydrolyze it into lactic acid, thus making milk a favorable medium for fermentation, since the pH of the milk falls and coagulates, and it may then be possible to produce dairy products, like cheese and yogurts. However, this requires controlled fermentation, as unwanted fermentation obviously results in the deterioration of milk [20].

Although lactose has many advantages for the food industry, this component of milk is also responsible for making it impossible for many people around the world to consume milk, since they have a lactose intolerance. The pathophysiological aspects or lifestyles that remove the consumption of milk by the population will be found in more detail in the next topic.

3. Adverse reactions to milk composition

Although milk is a good food source of compounds because it is associated with the supply of several essential nutrients to our diet, there are several concerns that must be taken into account for the consumption of this food, both in terms of different health problems and lifestyles that a person can manifest.

One of the adverse effects on human health is allergy to cow's milk protein, which occurs due to an adverse immune response to the cow's milk dietary antigen. The allergic process starts with casein, which makes up about 80% of milk proteins. When these proteins are digested, they are converted into opioid compounds called β-casomorphines that binds to the A1 allele of β-casein, thus causing allergy to the human body, especially in children and newborns, since your body does not yet recognize some proteins of cow's milk [21].

Another adverse cause that can be affected by the consumption of animal milk is lactose intolerance. This condition occurs when a person is unable to digest and absorb lactose from the diet. This is because there is a decline in lactase expression after weaning, commonly called "lactase non-persistence" [22].

Among the symptoms that identify lactose intolerance are gastrointestinal symptoms that can be presented with mild to moderate signs of indigestion, flatulence, nausea, diarrhea, and abdominal cramps after consumption of milk and dairy products [23].

Another factor that excludes animal milk from the diet, but that is not associated with any disease but with lifestyle is the case of vegans. The basic principle of vegetarianism is not consuming any type of red meat, chicken, or fish, but it may or may not include products of animal origin, such as eggs, milk and their derivates. Although it is often not very clear, veganism not only supports the exclusion of animal foods from its diet due to the animal's suffering, but also as a way of supporting the inclusion of plant foods produced by local producers that will present less environmental impact [5, 24].

Therefore, such conditions point to the need for not only animal milk but also its derivatives to obtain an alternative that is as healthy, so that people who cannot

DOI: http://dx.doi.org/10.5772/intechopen.94496

consume this food are also able to digest nutrients necessary for a good diet, in addition to presenting other food alternatives that allow you to diversify eating routines.

4. Plant-based milk alternatives

Currently, there are several researches for replacing milk using plant-based milk. This type of milk-like is a water-soluble extract based from vegetables, legumes, cereals, pseudocereals and nuts [25].

Vegetable milk processing can have several types of vegetable milk-like processing that will depend on the raw material from which this vegetable milk-like will be extracted. However, there are processing steps that are common to most vegetable milks, such as pre-treatment of raw material, extraction of milk, incorporation of additives, suspension, stabilization and adequate storage to improve shelf life of the product, as can be seen in **Figure 2** [26].

As it is still a studied product, there is still no concrete definition and classification in the literature of these plant-based milks. However, a general classification of these milk alternatives is divided into 5 subcategories, which are: cereal based, legume based, nut based, seed based and pseudocereal based [27].

In addition to providing lactose substitution, plant-based milks are also capable of providing health benefits to the general population and not only to those who should restrict lactose from the diet. This occurs because of the raw materials used in the production of these plant-based milks, since they have compounds that bring health benefits due to nutrients and micronutrients present in the composition of these foods that allow such beneficial actions to the human body.

Legumes are an important category in the divisions of vegetable milk, and chickpeas (*Cicer arietinum*) are rich in carbohydrates, proteins, vitamins, minerals, and fiber. Chickpeas have a high content of unsaturated fatty acids, such as linoleic acid (18: 2) and oleic acid (18: 1), and also have an excellent source of phosphorus, potassium, calcium, magnesium, sodium, iron, copper, manganese, and zinc [28].

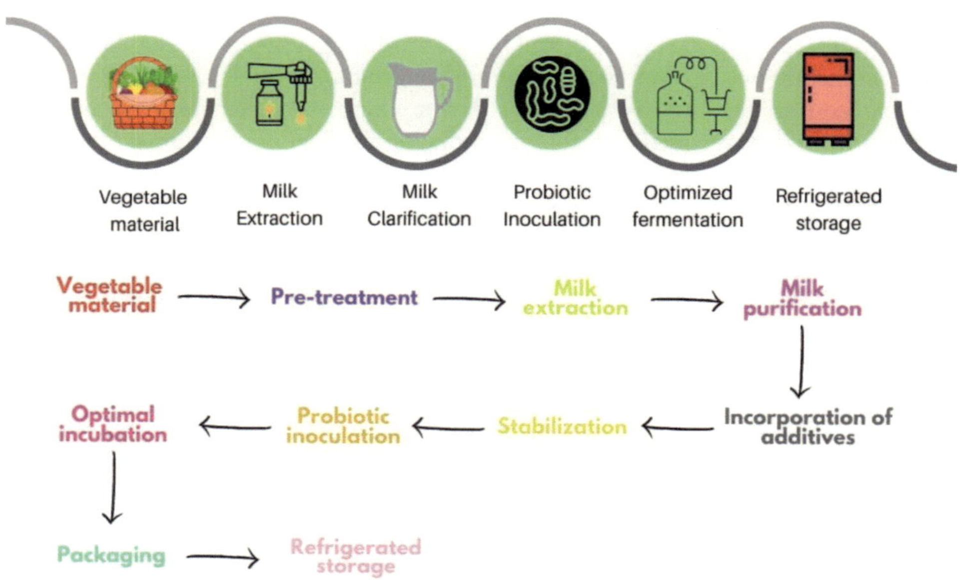

Figure 2.
Basic flow diagram to produce probiotic vegetable milk [26].

In chickpeas, polysaccharide (starch) is the largest component followed by fibers, contains monosaccharides (ribose, glucose, galactose, and fructose), disaccharides (sucrose, maltose), oligosaccharides (stachyose, ciceritol, raffinose, and verbascose) [29].

The fiber content of chickpeas in chickpeas is 18–22 g for every 100 g of raw material, with 4–8 g of soluble fibers and 10–18 g of insoluble fibers that are major players in cholesterol control total and LDL [30].

When chickpeas are cooked, they undergo ultrastructural changes that influence their nutritional, physical, and functional properties with significant decreases in antinutritional components and significant increases in dietary fibers and protein digestibility [31].

Chickpeas are a source of carbohydrates and proteins and can be used to develop products with greater added nutritional value, also, phytosterols present in the lipid fraction of chickpeas have antioxidant properties even at high temperatures [30, 32].

Soy (*Glycine max*) is rich in carbohydrates, proteins, and lipids. Soy milk is a good source of monounsaturated and polyunsaturated essential fatty acids, with significant amounts of polyunsaturated fatty acids, such as linoleic (18: 2) and linolenic acids (18: 3), has no cholesterol, and has a considerable content of vitamins and minerals. Soy milk is a good source of monounsaturated and polyunsaturated essential fatty acids. Soy protein is composed of all essential amino acids, many of which are present in quantities that correspond to those necessary for humans [5, 27].

Soy contains up to 35–45% protein and 20% fat and acts as an important source of protein, especially in people who follow a vegetarian diet. Due to its nutritional content, soy milk is used as a cow substitute for more than four decades. It also appears that the total number of calories available is comparable to a balanced nutritional profile [33].

Isoflavones appear to be the functionally active component responsible for the beneficial effects of soy. Isoflavones are well known for their protective effect against cancer, cardiovascular disease, and osteoporosis. Genistein is the most abundant isoflavone in soy and is considered the most biologically active [27].

Soy germination is known to be beneficial in reducing antinutrients as a trypsin inhibitor, phytic acid, flatulent, etc. Soy milk prepared by the traditional method presents some problems, many works and researches are trying to improve the quality by eliminating the strange taste and beans, inhibiting anti-nutritional factors, reducing the phytic acid content, improving the production of soy milk. All efforts generally address one or two of the associated problems and use heat-intensive methods to reduce antinutrients, thereby reducing the overall nutritional quality of soy milk. Germination, which is a natural non-thermal and non-chemical process, results in better quality processed products and soy germination would be an alternative to facilitate the development of products such as soy milk, which are usually prepared by heat treatment and moist protein-causing denaturation [34].

The pea (*Pisum sativum*) contains proteins that are easily digestible and has a high-quality amino acid profile, as well as a high content of lysine and arginine. Pea proteins have a very particular amino acid profile, different from other plant proteins. The amino acid profile of pea proteins is arginine, lysine, and branched-chain amino acids (isoleucine, leucine, and valine), glutamine, and glutamic acid [35].

Pea protein is a rich source of starch, fiber, vitamins, and minerals and easy to digest. Therefore, it can be used successfully as a substitute for animal protein in dairy products. Total pea proteins are divided into two main groups of albumin and globulins. However, pea's main storage proteins are often called legumin, vicilin, and convicilin, which make up the globulin fraction, which does not denature at different temperatures [36].

Lupine (*Lupinus termis*) is rich in alkaloids, amino acids, carbohydrates, and proteins with moderate gelatin properties compared to soy proteins. Lupine is a good source of nutrients, not just proteins, but also lipids, fibers, minerals, and vitamins. Lupines contain phytochemicals with antioxidant capacities, such as polyphenols, mainly tannins, and flavonoids [37].

With a high protein content of 25–40% can be used in milk-like products and substitutes, there is a growing interest in the production of lupine, due to its potential as a protein source, or for pharmaceutical purposes due to the high alkaline content, such as a natural component. Lupine milk-like plays a key role in meeting demand as an alternative to cow or human milk [37, 38].

Plant-based milks elaborated from seeds contain proteins that, like bovine milk proteins, tend to clot when they are acidified, heated, or enzymatically treated. Herewith, this type of vegetable milk-like is also capable of forming many products called "dairy products", such as creams, yogurts, ice cream and cheeses [39].

The most common types of vegetable milk-like produced from the seed is sesame milk. Sesame (*Sesamum indicum*) is a grain that contains high levels of phenolic compounds in their composition, which are considered with high antioxidant activity [40].

However, in sesame only a small amount of these components is present in their free form, the remainder being linked to glucose in the form of mono/di/tri-glucoside lignan, thus not exercising its antioxidant activity. However, when fermenting sesame milk-like with a lactic acid β-glucosidase, the glycoside bonds are broken resulting in a compound called aglycone, which increases the product's antioxidant activity [41].

Because of this, initially, only sesame milk-like may not be considered an advantageous vegetable milk-like when compared to other plant-based milks, but in application of yogurts and fermented beverages, this food can have great nutritional advantages.

Another type of seed that can be used to elaborated vegetable milk is pumpkin seed (*Cucurbita maxima* Linn*)*. This seed is widely consumed in the form of snacks in different regions of the word, but due to its nutritional advantages, it has been thought about its use in the development of other types of products [42].

This seed is an important nutritional source, as it contains lipids (30.66%), protein (33.48%) and carbohydrate (28.68%). Still, its extract proved to be effective against diabetes and hypercholesterolemia due to the components present in its composition [43].

Flaxseed is a food rich in all essential fatty acids, especially omega-3 that is responsible for increased immunity and brain function. In addition, it has amino acids that are responsible for maintaining proper cellular function through the synthesis of protein. As a result, flaxseed has gained presence in research for the development of vegetable milks-like since its use improves the nutritional quality of the final product [44].

Another subcategory of plant-based milks is those obtained from pseudocereals, such as Quinoa *(Chenopodium quinoa* Willd.), a plant that belongs to the *Chenopodiaceae* family. Because it has a high amount of protein and an adequate balance of amino acids, this plant has been considered of great importance, especially for individuals who do not, or make little intake of foods rich in proteins and amino acids such as meat, eggs and milk [45].

Despite its great nutritional advantages, quinoa is still not a widely used food for developing new types of food products, as it has a high cost when compared to other types of food available, especially in the case of the development of plant-based milks-like [46].

Cereals are another subcategory that can develop a vegetable milk-like. Although there are countless cereals present around the word, the most common types of vegetable milk-like obtained from cereals are rice and oats.

Oat (*Avena sativa* L.) is a specie of cereal grain rich in biological substances, such as soluble dietary fiber, β-glucan, vitamin E and polyunsaturated fatty acids that make the consumption of this food of great importance for human health in the long term [47].

Among the components present in oats, β-glucan is the most important since this component has a prebiotic function in the gastrointestinal tract supporting the growth of microorganisms beneficial to our body; In addition, β-glucan moderates the glycemic response of the oat starch portion. In addition, this cereal contains several bioactive phytochemical, such as, for example, phenolic acids, flavonoids, carotenoids and phytosterols, in addition to the avenanthramides and steroidal saponins, which are found exclusively in this food [48, 49].

Although rice is low in protein, it is still a food to be taken into account for the production of plant-based milks, due to its underutilization and high nutrient profile. A natural fermentation with lactic acid bacteria there is a break in the antinutritional factors that cause an increase in the content of calcium, iron and magnesium, causing the beneficial bacteria in our gastrointestinal tract to collaborate in digestion and in the immunity of other internal organs [50].

Therefore, the use of isolated rice milk-like may not appear to be of any benefit, but when subjected to a fermentation process, which occurs in the production of many dairy products, this vegetable milk-like can have positive advantages for the final product.

Another subcategory that can be found to produce vegetable milk are nuts. Almond (*Prunus dulcis*) has as main components proteins, lipids, soluble sugars, minerals, and fibers. Most almonds are fatty, between 35 and 52%, followed by protein, 22 to 25%, with lipids mainly as unsaturated fatty acids and proteins as essential amino acids. Also they are rich in nutrients such as calcium, magnesium, selenium, potassium, zinc, phosphorus, and copper and, due to the presence of arabinose, they have prebiotic properties [5].

Almonds are rich in monounsaturated fatty acids (MUFA), which are considered useful for weight loss and control. There is also much convincing evidence that MUFA helps to reduce the content of low-density lipoproteins (LDL) in the blood. Almonds are also an essential source of various nutrients, including protein, fiber, vitamin E, manganese, and antioxidants, and are therefore reflected in almond milk-like. Its consumption has beneficial effects on human health, and it is especially related to the blood lipid profile and the risk of cardiovascular diseases [33].

Coconut (*Cocos nucifera*) milk-like can increase HDL (high-density lipoprotein) levels, which helps to reduce harmful LDL (low-density lipoprotein). Coconut fats have lauric fatty acid, which mainly contributes to increasing HDL cholesterol levels, which helps to lower LDL cholesterol levels in the bloodstream [33].

Coconut milk-like is used as a milk substitute (cow's milk) in dairy products such as cheese, yoghurt, chocolate, and frozen dessert. In this way, coconut milk is considered one of the most suitable substitutes for milk. Therefore, milk and coconut milk can serve as substitutes for each other, depending on the purpose of the substitution [51].

Young coconut milk contains carbohydrates (mainly sucrose and some starch), lipids, and minerals, such as phosphorus, calcium, and potassium. Coconut protein is rich in lysine, methionine, and tryptophan. Coconut water extracted from young coconuts has a pleasant taste and balance of sodium, potassium, calcium, and magnesium since many plant extracts are mixed with the water of the coconut itself for yield and stability [52].

Milk alternative	Subcategory	Health benefits	Author, year
Oat Milk	Cereal	It has an anti-carcinogenic component and reduces LDL cholesterol levels; Rich in fibers, antioxidants and polyphenols.	Paul; Kumar; Sharma, 2019 [50]
Soy Milk	Legume	Source of essential fatty acids, considered good for cardiovascular health; Therapeutic properties and protective roles against several age-related diseases.	Nawaz, et al., 2020 [53]
Almond Milk	Nuts	Rich in monounsaturated fatty acids, which help in weight management and can lower LDL cholesterol	Vanga, et al., 2020 [54]
Quinoa Milk	Pseudocereal	Contains all essential amino acids and high quality fatty acids; Contains minerals and amino acids that help in memory and reducing anxiety in stressful situations.	Bianchi, et al., 2014 [55]

Table 2.
Examples of raw materials in vegetable milks-like and their health benefits.

A summary of health benefits provided by the different raw materials used in the production of vegetable milk-like is presented in **Table 2**.

5. Use of milk substitutes in dairy products

Currently, there are not many researches focused on the use of plant-based milks in the production of dairy products such as fermented beverages, ice cream, yoghurt and cheese, for example. Despite this, the work that has been carried out in this area produces results that help not only to improve previous research but also to conduct new research and new products at the market.

Recently, a fermented beverage produced from lentil grains fermented with *Lactobacillus* strain was evaluated in order to analyze its biochemical and nutritional composition, in addition to the viable cell count during its storage time. The work concluded through the obtained results that the protocol used showed to have adequate potential for applications in other types of fermented beverages and with the possibility of using other types of legumes [56].

Adding the nutritional value of the legumes, and their generated vegetable extract, it can lead to the production of ice cream, with soy extract and soybean protein, with functional properties, that also impose specific structural characteristics of product. With the obtained results it is possible to conclude that the use of soy for the preparation of gelato shows differentiating characteristics in terms of protein content, solubility and viscosity of the final product, which is also well accepted by consumers [57].

An alternative to soy milk-like was made by the production of fresh and fermented chickpeas, producing plant-based beverages. The fresh chickpeas presents a good result in the nutritional and organoleptic quality of the product, being a potential substitute for soy in plant-based beverages, although further research is necessary to minimize the syneresis of the elaborated product [58].

Texture properties are related to sensory acceptance by consumers. Vegetable yogurts based on oats is possible, nevertheless the perception of the plant-based yoghurt in the mouth has greater variation compared to traditional yoghurt, due to its textural properties, such as thickness and creaminess inferior to the product elaborated with animal milk. Therefore, to be acceptable by consumers, it is recommended that its final texture properties be considered during the product development phase [59].

Another oat base to produce a fermented product like the traditional yoghurt can be used, leading to acceptable appearance and taste. However, is necessary to evaluate the physical and nutritional quality of products [60].

Ice creams fermented with *Lactobacillus acidophilus* (Bb-12) and *Bifidobacterium bifidum* (La-05) can be prepared from cow's milk, soy, or coconut, as well as the combination of cow's milk or coconut milk (1 = 25%, 2 = 50% and 3 = 75%) with soy milk (75%, 50%, and 25% respectively). The substitution of cow's milk for soy and coconut milk increase the probiotic growth of (Bb-12) and (La-05), thus showing that soy and coconut vegetable milk-like ice creams provide a richer growth in amino acids and sugars for Bb12- and La-05 than cow's milk. Thus, ice creams produced with plant extracts can be a good vehicle to deliver probiotic content [61].

Cow's milk can be replaced by soy and coconut milk-like, and various combinations with cow's milk for producing ice creams. The addition of vegetable milk-like increases the pH and decreased the melting rate, varying the viscosity and particle size [62].

In the development of technological products based on vegetable milk-like, the production of desserts with chocolate based on yams and rice, a difference on textural properties can be found. In comparison with products produced with animal milk such as *brigadeiro* (typical Brazilian desert), a difference in flavor is observed, due to the lack of some components of the plant extract, such as low-fat content. Among the chocolate desserts, the rice based presents a mild starchy flavor, which can end up providing less acceptance by consumers. The coconut-based dessert, with rice milk-like and yam, can stood out for its flavor and characteristics [63].

Curd can be developed by substituting cow's milk for different plant extracts such as oats, rice, and almonds, adding *Lactobacillus* sp. Milk-like and curd from almond can be highly acceptable, with adequate pH and nutritious values. Milk-like and curd developed from plant sources may represent safe food as part of diet for people with lactose intolerance [64].

Yoghurt is an excellent probiotic source and because of that, when using a plant-based milk substitute for yoghurt production, it is interesting to consider whether such beverages are capable of maintain the minimum required of the population that are responsible for maintaining the probiotic characteristics of this type of product, as it was analyzed in a developed work, in which yogurts were produced using a vegetable beverages made from soy, rice and coconut. With the results achieved, it was possible to conclude that not only fermented beverages, but also non-fermented ones are able to supply and transport lactic acid bacteria and also other microorganisms, even without the fermentation process and subjecting the products to storage under refrigeration. Thus indicating that a yoghurt produced from a plant-based beverage is also capable of promoting desirable characteristics for consumers for this type of product, thus promoting a wider range of plant-based dairy derivatives also for consumers who are unfit to consume dairy derivatives from animal sources [65].

The effect of syneresis on yoghurt is very important for evaluating the final product. Because of this, it is very important to evaluate this property of a yoghurt elaborated with plant extract. Therefore, a work evaluated the effect of storing a yoghurt elaborated from a plant extract on the syneresis of yoghurt and concluded that this property increased as the storage time passed and that the syneresis is inversely related to the pH of the product, thus being in agreement with other related works [66].

As noted, soy is the most used food and cited in research to replace milk and the use of plant extracts. A work conducted a functional and physical analysis of a product fermented using soy extract, fermented with a probiotic culture of kefir, and with added soy fiber and the results concluded that the product elaborated with the addition of fiber was firmer and with a lower syneresis value when compared to the product elaborated without the added fiber. With this, the product can be considered as an alternative to the existing products on the market, since, in addition to presenting such advantages even at the end of the storage analysis period, it presented an adequate probiotic culture count to be considered as a functional product [67].

Currently, a greater demand for symbiotic products, that is, those in which there is a combination of probiotic and prebiotic means has been offered to consumers in order to benefit human health. Therefore, several studies have developed products with symbiotic characteristics also for consumers who are unable to consume animal milk, and therefore, they use plant extracts to produce such analogs.

A work developed a symbiotic oat-based beverage, produced with a probiotic culture (*L.plantarum*) and prebiotic product (inulin) in order to evaluate its physical–chemical properties and its probiotic survival. Therefore, the work concluded that the probiotic culture of the product remained with adequate values for food during its storage period and its physical–chemical analysis showed a product with a low fat content and a high content of dietary fiber, being then a healthy alternative to be presented to consumers [68].

6. Conclusions

Although animal milk is a very important food for the human diet due to its supply of essential nutrients, which in some cases are not found in other foods, the use of vegetable milk-like is a viable alternative to offer consumers who cannot or do not choose to consume animal milk.

Therefore, plant-based milk substitutes have gained market share, as they are beneficial to health due to the raw materials that are used in their production. However, in the development field, much research must still be carried out for the formulation its products, since there is still not much works mainly in the elaboration of vegetable milk based dairy derivatives, improving the offer and the consumption options for the population.

Conflict of interest

The authors declare no conflict of interest.

Author details

Laís Zandona, Caroline Lima and Suzana Lannes*
Pharmaceutical-Biochemical Technology Department, Pharmaceutical Sciences School, University of Sao Paulo, Sao Paulo, Brazil

*Address all correspondence to: scslan@usp.br

References

[1] LU A. Dairy, Science, Society, and the Environment. Oxford Research Encyclopedia of Environmental Science. 2017; 1-64. DOI: 10.1093/acrefore/9780199389414.013.316

[2] Zimmermann P, Curtis, N. Breast milk microbiota: a review of the factors that influence composition. Journal of Infection. 2020; 81:17-47. DOI: 10.1016/j.jinf.2020.01.023

[3] Belitz H D, Grosch P, Schieberle P. Milk and Dairy Products. In: Belitz H D, Grosch P, Schieberle, P, editors. Food Chemistry. 4th ed. Heidelberg: Springer; 2008. p. 498-521. DOI: 10.1007/978-3-540-69934-7_11

[4] Muehlhoff E, Bennett A, Macmahon D. Milk and dairy products in human nutrition. Rome: FAO – Food and Agriculture Organization of the United Nations. Available in: http://www.fao.org/3/i3396e/i3396e.pdf. Last accessed in September 2020.

[5] Silva A R A, Silva M M N, Ribeiro B D. Health issues and technological aspects of plant-based alternative milk. Food Research International. 2020; 131: 1-17. DOI: 10.1016/j.foodres.2019.108972

[6] Alves M P, et. al. Chapter 6 – Alternative Processing Procedures and Technological Advantages of Raw Milk. In: Nero L A, Carvalho, A F de, editors. Raw Milk: Balance Between Hazards and Benefits. 1st ed. Cambridge: Academic Press; 2019. p. 117-125. DOI: 10.1016/B978-0-12-810530-6.00006-7

[7] Deeth H C. Chapter 10 – The effect of UHT processing and storage on milk proteins. In: Boland M, Singh H, editors. Milk Proteins: From Expression to Food. 3rd ed. Cambridge: Academic Press; 2020. p. 385-421. DOI: 10.1016/B978-0-12-815251-5.00010-4

[8] Dohtre A V. Milk Pasteurization and Equipment. In: Mandal P K, Biswas, A K, editors. Animal Products Technology. 1st ed. Delhi: Studium Press; 2014. p. 51-78.

[9] Rafiq S M, Rafiq S I. Milk by-products Utilization. In: Ibrahim S A, Zimmerman T, Gyawali R, editors. Current Issues and Challenges in the Dairy Industry. 1st ed. London: Intechopen; 2020. p. 1-8. DOI: 10.5772/intechopen.85533

[10] Burke N, et. al. The Dairy Industry: Process, Monitoring, Standards, and Quality. In: Díaz A V, García-Gimeno R M, editors. Descriptive Food Science. 1st ed. London: Intechopen; 2018. p. 3-25. DOI: 10.5772/intechopen.80398

[11] Claeys W L, et. al. Consumption of raw or heated milk from different species: An evaluation of the nutritional and potential health benefits. Food Control. 2014; 42:188-201. DOI: 10.1016/j.foodcont.2014.01.045

[12] Mourad G, Samir M, Bettache G. Composition, and nutritional value of raw milk. Issues in Biological Sciences and Pharmaceutical Research. 2014; 2:115-122. DOI: 10.15739/ibspr.005

[13] Poppit S D. Chapter 18 – Milk proteins and human health. In: Boland M, Singh H, editors. Milk Proteins: From Expression to Food. 3rd ed. Cambridge: Academic Press; 2020; p. 651-669. DOI: 10.1016/B978-0-12-815251-5.00018-9

[14] O'Callaghan T F, et. al. Chapter 7 – Nutritional Aspects of Raw Milk: A Beneficial or Hazardous Food Choice. In: Nero L A, Carvalho, A F de, editors. Raw Milk: Balance Between Hazards and Benefits. 1st ed. Cambridge: Academic Press; 2019; p. 127-148. DOI: 10.1016/B978-0-12-810530-6.00007-9

[15] Kalyankar S D, et. al. Milk: Sources and Composition. Encyclopedia of Food and Health. 2016; 741-747. DOI: 10.1016/B978-0-12-384947-2.00463-3

[16] Pereira, P C. Milk nutritional composition and its role in human health. Nutrition. 2014; 30:619-627. DOI: 10.1016/j.nut.2013.10.011

[17] Lecomte M, Bourlieu C, Michalski, M-C. Chapter 35 – Nutritional properties of Milk Lipids: Specific Function of the Milk Fat Globule. In: Watson R R, Collier R J, Preedy, V R, editors. Dairy in Human Health and Disease Across Lifespan. 1st ed. Cambridge: Academic Press; 2017; p. 435-452. DOI: 10.1016/B978-0-12-809868-4.00035-2

[18] Gómez-Cortés P, Juárez M, Fuente M G de la. Milk fatty acids and potential health benefits: An updated vision. Trends in Food Science & Technology. 2018; 81:1-9. DOI: 10.1016/j.tifs.2018.08.014

[19] Renhe I R T, et. al. Chapter 2 – Physicochemical Characteristics of Raw Milk. In: Nero L A, Carvalho, A F de, editors. Raw Milk: Balance Between Hazards and Benefits. 1st ed. Cambridge: Academic Press; 2019; p. 29-43. DOI: 10.1016/B978-0-12-810530-6.00002-X

[20] Kelly A L, Larsen L B. 1 – Milk Biochemistry. In: Griffiths M W, editor. Improving the Safety and Quality of Milk: Milk Production and Processing. 1st ed. Sawston: Woodhead Publishing; 2010; p. 3-26. DOI: 10.1533/9781845699420.1.3

[21] Rangel A H N, et. al. Lactose intolerance and cow's milk protein allergy. Food Science Technology. 2016; 36:179-187. DOI: 10.1590/1678-457X.0019

[22] Heine R G, et. al. Lactose intolerance and gastrointestinal cow's milk allergy in infants and children – common misconceptions revisited. Word Allergy Organization Journal. 2017; 10:2-8. DOI: 10.1186/s40413-017-0173-0

[23] Brian Orr B A, et. al. 21 – Lactose Intolerance Testing. In: Pizzorno J E, Murray M T, editors. Textbook of Natural Medicine. 5th ed. London: Churchill Livingstone; 2020; p. 182-186. DOI: 10.1016/B978-0-323-43044-9.00021-2

[24] Walsh M C, Gunn C. Chapter 13 – Non-dairy milk substitutes: Are they of adequate nutritional composition? In: Givens D I, editor. Milk and Dairy Foods: Their functionality in Human Health and Disease. 1st ed. Cambridge: Academic Press; 2020; p. 347-369. DOI: 10.1016/B978-0-12-815603-2.00013-9

[25] Astolfi M L, et. al. Comparative elemental analysis of dairy milk and plant-based milk alternatives. Food Control. 2020; 116:1-11. DOI: 10.1016/j.foodcont.2020.107327

[26] Kehinde B A, et. al. Chapter Four – Vegetable milk as probiotic and prebiotic foods. In: Cruz A G Prudencio E S, Esmerino E A, Silva M C da, editors. Probiotic and Prebiotics in Foods: Challanges, Innovations and Advances. 1st ed. Cambridge: Academic Press; 2020; p. 115-160. DOI: 10.1016/bs.afnr.2020.06.003

[27] Sethi S, Tyagi S K, Anurag R K. Plant-based milk alternatives an emerging segment of functional beverages: A review. Journal of Food Science and Technology. 2016; 53: 3408-3423. DOI: 10.1007/s13197-016-2328-3

[28] Ferreira A C P, Brazaca S G C, Arthur V. Alterações químicas e nutricionais do grão de bico (*Cicer arietinum L.)* cru irradiado e submetido à cocção. Food Science and Technology. 2006; 26: 80-88. DOI: 10.1590/S0101-20612006000100014.

[29] Jukanti A K, et. al. Nutritional quality and health benefits of chickpea *(Cicer arietinum L.)*: a review. British Journal of Nutrition. 2012; 108: 11:26. DOI: 10.1017/S0007114512000797

[30] Kishor K, et. al. Nutritional Composition of Chickpea *(Cicer arietinum)* Milk. International Journal of Chemical Studies. 2017; 5: 1941-1944.

[31] Xu Y, Thomas M, Bhardwaj H L. Chemical composition, functional properties and microstructural characteristics of three kabuli chickpea (*Cicer arietinum L.*) as affected by different cooking methods. International Journal of Food Science & Technology. 2014; 49: 1215-1223. DOI: 10.1111/ijfs.12419

[32] Hirdyani H. Nutritional composition of chickpea (*Cicerarietinum-L)* and value-added products. Indian Journal of Community Health. 2014; 26: 102-106.

[33] Vanga S K, Raghavan V. How well do plant-based alternatives fare nutritionally compared to cow's milk? Journal of Food Science and Technology. 2018; 55: 10-20. DOI: 10.1007/s13197

[34] Murugkar D A. Effect of sprouting of soybean on the chemical composition and quality of soymilk and tofu. Journal of Food Science and Technology. 2014; 51: 915-921. DOI: 10.1007/s13197-011

[35] Yousseef M, et. al. Fermentation of cow milk and/or pea milk mixtures by different starter cultures: Physico-chemical and sensorial properties. LWT – Food Science and Technology. 2016; 69: 430-437

[36] Khiabanian N O, et. al. Chemical, textural, rheological, and sensorial properties of wheyless feta cheese as influenced by replacement of milk protein concentrate with pea protein isolate. Journal of Texture Studies. 2020; 51: 488-500. DOI: 10.1111/jtxs.12508

[37] Awad R A, Salama W S, Farahat A M. Effect of lupine as cheese base substitution on technological and nutritional properties of processed cheese analogue. Acta Scientiarum Polonorum Technologia Alimentaria. 2014; 13: 55-64. DOI: 10.17306/j.afs.2014.1.5.

[38] Mohamed S A, et. al. Production of vegetable yoghurt like from lupine milk. Arab Universities Journal of Agricultural Sciences. 2019; 27: 2155-2165. DOI: 10.21608/ajs.2019.15670.1069

[39] McClements, D J, Newman E, McClements I F. Plant-based milks: A Review of the Science Underpinning Their Design, Fabrication, and Performance. Comprehensive Reviews in Food Science and Food Safety. 2019; 18: 2047-2067. DOI: 10.1111/1541-4337.12505

[40] Shahidi F, Liyana-Pathirana C M, Wall D S. Antioxidant activity of white and black sesame seeds and their hull fractions. Food Chemistry. 2006; 99: 478-483. DOI: 10.1016/j.foodchem.2005.08.009

[41] Fitrotin U, et. al. Antioxidant Properties of Fermented Sesame Milk Using *Lactobacillus plantarum* Dad 13. International Research Journal of Biological Sciences. 2015; 4: 56-61.

[42] Karaye I U, et. al. Evaluation of Nutrient and Anti-nutrient Contents of Selected Nigerian Cucurbits Seeds. Research Journal of Pharmaceutical, Biological and Chemical Sciences. 2013; 4: 137-142

[43] Habib A, et. al. Nutritional and Lipid Composition Analysis of Pumpkin Seed (*Cucurbita maxima Linn.)*. Journal of Nutrition & Food Sciences. 2015; 5: 1-6. DOI: 10.4172/2155-9600.1000374

[44] Senila L, et. al. Chemical, Nutritional and Antioxidant Characteristics of Different Food Seeds.

Applied Sciences. 2020; 10: 1-16. DOI: 10.3390/app1005189

[45] Navruz-Varli S, Sanlier N. Nutritional and health benefits of quinoa (*Chenopodium quinoa* Willd.). Journal of Cereal Science. 2016; 69: 371-376. DOI: 10.1016/j.jcs2016.05.004

[46] Marandini-Filho A M. Quinoa: Nutritional Aspects. Journal of Nutraceuticals and Food Science. 2017; 2: 1-5.

[47] El-Batawy O I, Mahdy S M, Gohari S T. Development of Functional Fermented Oat Milk by Using Probiotic Strains and Whey Protein. International Journal of Dairy Science. 2019; 14: 21-28. DOI: 10.3923/ijds.2019.21.28

[48] Ravindran S, RadhaiSri S. Probiotic oats milk with microencapsulated *Lactobacillus plantarum* – an alternative to dairy products. Nutrition & Food Science. 2020; 1: 1-12. DOI: 10.1108/NFS-03-2020-0073

[49] Sang S, Chu Y. Whole grain oats, more than just a fiber: Role of unique phytochemicals. Molecular Nutrition & Food Research. 2017; 61: 1-12. DOI: 10.1002/mnfr.201600715

[50] Paul A A, et. al. Milk analog: Plant based alternatives to conventional milk, production, potential, and health concerns. Critical Reviews in Food Science and Nutrition. 2019; 1: 1-19. DOI: 10.1080/10408398.2019.1674243

[51] Marina A M, NurulAzizah S. Use of coconut versus dairy milk products in Malaysian Dishes: Comparison of Nutritional composition and sensory evaluation. Journal of Food and Nutritional Research. 2014; 2: 204-208. DOI: 10.12691/jfnr-2-4-12.

[52] Yuliana N, Rangga A, Rakhmiati. Manufacture of fermented coco milk-drink containing lactic acid bacteria cultures. African Journal of Food Science. 2010; 4: 558-562.

[53] Nawaz M D, et. al. An emerging segment of functional legume-based beverages: a review. Food Reviews International. 2020; 1: 1-39. DOI: 10.1080/87559129.2020.1762641

[54] Vanga S K, et. al. Effect of pulsed ultrasound, a green food processing technique, on the secondary structure and *in-vitro* digestibility of almond milk protein. Food Research International. 2020; 137: 1-7. DOI: 10.1016/j.foodres.2020.109523

[55] Bianchi F, et. al. Potentially symbiotic fermented beverage with aqueous extracts of quinoa (*Cheopodium quinoa* Willd) and soy. Food Science and Technology International. 2014; 21: 403-415. DOI: 10.1177/1082013214540672

[56] Verni M, et. al. Design and Characterization of a Novel Fermented Beverage from Lentil Grains. Foods. 2020; 9: 1-13. DOI: 10.3390/foods9070893

[57] Savio J, et. al. Development and Structural Behavior of Soybean Gelato. Food Technology and Biotechnology. 2018; 56: 1-19. DOI: 10.17113/ftb.56.04.18.5710

[58] Wang S, Chelikani V, Serventi L. Evaluation of chickpea as alternative to soy in plant-based beverages, fresh and fermented. LWT – Food Science and Technology. 2018; 97: 570-572. DOI: 10.1016/j.lwt.2018.07.067

[59] Greis M, et. al. Dynamic texture perception in plant-based yogurt alternatives: Identifying temporal drivers of liking by TDS. Food Quality and Preference. 2020; 86: 1-10. DOI: 10.1016/j.foodqual.2020.104019

[60] Martensson O, et. al. Formulation of an oat-based fermented product and its comparison with yoghurt. Journal of the Science of Food and Agriculture. 2001; 81: 1314-1321. DOI: 10.1002/jsfa.947

[61] Aboulfazli F, Shori A B, Baba A S. Effects of the replacement of cow milk with vegetable milk on probiotics and nutritional profile of fermented ice cream. LWT – Food Science and Technology. 2016; 70: 261-270. DOI: 10.1016/j.lwt.2016.02.056

[62] Aboulfazli F, Baba A S, Misran M. Effect of Vegetable Milks on the Physical and Rheological Properties of Ice Cream. Food Science and Technology Research. 2014; 20: 987-996. DOI: 10.3136/fstr.20.987

[63] Siqueri T M, et. al. Desenvolvimento de produtos tecnológicos a base de leite vegetal. Competência Técnica e Responsabilidade Social e Ambiental nas Ciências Agrárias 2. 2020; 1: 129-137. DOI: 10.22533/at.ed.42420220115

[64] Rai S R, Pachisia J, Singh S. A Study on the Acceptability of Plant-Based Milk and Curd among the Lactose Intolerant People Residing in Kolkata. 2018; 8: 38-43.

[65] Zareba D, Malgorzata Z. The viability of yoghurt bacteria in selected plant beverages. Zesyty Problemowe Postepów Nauk Rolniczych. 2017; 591: 87-96. DOI: 10.22630/ZPPNR.2017.591.46

[66] Panesar P S, Shind C. Effect of storage on Syneresis, pH, *Lactobacillus acidophilus* Count, *Bifidobacterium bifidum* count of *Aloe vera* fortified probiotic yoghurt. Current Research in Dairy Sciences. 2012; 4: 17-23. DOI: 10.3923/crds.2012.17.23

[67] Baú T R, Garcia S, Ida E I. Evaluation of a functional soy product with addition of soy fiber and fermented with probiotic kefir culture. Brazilian archives of biology and technology: an international journal. 2014; 57: 402-409. DOI: 10.1590/S1516-89132014005000005

[68] Wang C, et al. Physiochemical properties and probiotic survivability of symbiotic oat-based beverage. Food science and Biotechnology. 2017; 27: 735-743. DOI: 10.1007/s10068-017-0290-0

Chapter 2

Production and Consumer Acceptance of Millet Beverages

Patrycja Cichońska and Małgorzata Ziarno

Abstract

The use of millet for the production of plant-based beverages has beneficial effects because it is healthy and gluten-free. In its raw form, millet is rich in dietary fiber and polyphenols. Millet beverages are characterized by relatively low popularity among the consumers of plant beverages. This is mainly due to the drawbacks, namely the presence of plant flavors and "millet" smell. Constant market growth requires new products to be developed in order to meet the consumers' expectations. The acceptance of millet beverages significantly increases when these are offered in various flavors. Furthermore, the addition of apple or banana puree to millet recipes can increase their desirability. Stabilization of millet beverages is important as they have the tendency to delaminate. This can be overcome by the use of natural stabilizers such as pectin and agar-agar which seems to be an effective option for these products.

Keywords: millet, plant-based beverages, recipe, consumer preferences, milk analogues

1. Introduction

Plant-based beverages are a group of products that are continuously gaining significant interest in the food market every year. These products are becoming popular for many reasons. They are mostly used as a vegan substitute for cow's milk by consumers who restrict or exclude animal products in their diets. This is due to the increasing awareness of the society about the impact of intensive animal husbandry on the climate, as well as the health benefits of using plant-based diets. In addition, beverages prepared from plants are consumed by people who have food allergies and intolerances to specific milk components. They also add great variety to the daily diet.

One of the plant beverages less appreciated among consumers is the millet beverage. Millet is a cereal that has a similar nutritional value as the most popular crops such as wheat and rye. It is highly resistant to high temperatures, drought, and pest activities. Millet products are gluten-free and hence suitable for consumption by people suffering from gluten allergy or intolerance.

Millet is rich in health-promoting ingredients, such as fiber, polyphenols, minerals (including copper, phosphorus, iron), and B vitamins. Consumption of this product can have a positive effect on human health. Millet beverages are yet to become popular among consumers because of their low sensory acceptability. Constant growth of the assortment of plant-based beverages and their increased availability has led to a need to develop new products and improve the existing ones to meet consumers' needs and expectations.

2. Millet beverage and its consumer acceptance

2.1 Characteristics of millet and its products

Millet (*Panicum* L.) is a plant belonging to a family of grasses that consists of several species of annual plants and perennials. It is one of the oldest cereal plants, originating from the regions of India and Central Asia. The most cultivated millet variety is common millet (*Panicum miliaceum* L.). Millet crops have been known and used probably as early as 7000 or 6000 BC, and are therefore considered as one of the earliest cultivated grain grasses. Since that time, their advantages such as resistance to drought and a relatively short period of maturation have been known, despite the high cultivation of their competitors, wheat and barley. Originally grown in northern China or the Caucasus, millets have spread in all directions and have even reached Europe. Millet is the major food for several people living in hot and dry areas around the world. It is mainly grown in marginal agricultural areas where there are low yields of major crops such as wheat and maize due to poor rainfall. In addition, millet is an important source of carbohydrate and protein for millions of people living in Africa. It is the sixth most cultivated cereal in terms of global agricultural production. The largest producers of millet are India, Nigeria, Niger, and China. Furthermore, millet is resistant to pests and has a short cultivation period compared to major cereals [1, 2].

Owing to its technological and health benefits, millet grains are gaining increasing interest among food technologists and nutritionists every year. Millet-based dishes, beverages, and snacks are known all over the world; however, the grain still dominates only in African countries. Millet has a high nutritional value, which is comparable to the macronutrient content in the seeds of major cereals such as wheat, maize, or rice. **Table 1** compares the nutritional values of different types of cereal grains. These values vary depending on the cereal variety. Millet proteins are a good source of essential amino acids, except for lysine and threonine; however, they are relatively rich in methionine [1–3].

The distribution of macronutrients in millet is similar to that in major cereals; therefore, millet is recognized as a suitable raw material for use in the industrial production of snacks, dietary foods, or baby food. Millet grains require proper processing before consumption. The most popular methods used for its processing are hulling, grinding, flaking, polishing, fermentation, and soaking. These methods improve the nutritional and sensory properties of millet, which includes an increase in the bioavailability of micronutrients and a decrease in the content of antinutritional substances, such as phytic acid. **Table 2** shows a comparison of the average

Type of cereal	Carbohydrates [g/100 g]		Protein [g/100 g]	Fat [g/100 g]
	Starch and sugars	Roughage		
Wheat	60.0–75.0	2.0–3.0	10.0–25.0	2.0–2.6
Rye	65.0–73.2	1.6–2.7	7.2–16.0	1.5–2.3
Barley	68.0–78.0	4.5–7.2	10.5–16.3	1.9–2.6
Oat	31.1–51.0	7.7–19.2	9.0–19.0	3.1–6.6
Maize	68.0–78.0	2.0–3.0	9.0–13.0	4.0–6.0
Millet	58.0–82.0	3.2–11.4	9.8–17.2	1.9–4.8
Rice	65.0–80.0	7.8–12.5	7.0–10.8	1.2–2.5

Table 1.
Comparison of the nutritional value of cereal grains [2, 3].

Type of product	Carbohydrates [g/100 g]		Protein [g/100 g]	Fat [g/100 g]
	Starch and sugars	Roughage		
Millet	70.0	7.3	13.5	3.3
Millet flour	78.7	5.9	12.1	3.6
Millet flakes	80.5	3.8	8.1	3.2
Millet groats	71.6	3.2	11.3	2.9

Table 2.
Comparison of the average nutritional value of millet and its products [3, 4].

nutritional value of millet and its products. However, industrial processing is not effective, which often negatively affects the properties of this cereal (e.g. reduction in the nutrient content of the product compared to its raw material) [2].

One of the millet processing methods is hulling. The millet grains are small in size compared to other cereals; therefore, to facilitate hulling, millet is first subjected to a hydrothermal treatment. This treatment contributes to the hardening of its endosperm, the inner tissue of the seed containing nutrient reserves. Shelled millet can be cooked to obtain a soft and edible structure in a short time. However, hulling reduces some of the nutrients in the product, such as dietary fiber, minerals, and polyphenols [1, 2].

In order to obtain millet flour, whole or previously dehulled millet grains are subjected to a milling process. Earlier dehulling removes the bran, which simultaneously reduces the amount of fiber, minerals, and antioxidants in the flour, resulting in an overall reduction in the nutritional value of the product. The use of whole grains to produce flour is therefore more beneficial from a health perspective [2].

Millet flakes are another product obtained by processing. First, millet grains are moistened and directed to the evaporator, where they are subjected to steam under pressure for several minutes. After evaporation, the grains are left to mature and then directed to the roller mill. The crusher reduces the grains to thin flakes with certain moisture content (usually 17–18%). The obtained flakes are dried on a belt dryer at a temperature of approximately 50 degrees Celsius. The dried flakes are then cooled down and sorted properly [5].

To obtain groats from millet, the tegument is removed from the grain and then the hulled grains are polished. Millet groats are known not only for their sensory properties and wide range of use but also for their nutritional value. Groats are an excellent source of energy (starch makes up 65% of the product's weight), plant proteins, magnesium, zinc, and B vitamins (mainly thiamine and riboflavin) [5, 6].

Fermentation is widely used in parts of Africa, mainly because of the low popularity of the other methods of food preservation. This process not only extends the shelf life of a product but also improves its nutritional value and increases the range of products available. Fermented foods are consumed all over the world for their health benefits, but unfortunately fermented millet products are not popular in Europe. Such foods are obtained by the colonization of plants by specific bacterial microflora, whose enzymes (including amylases, proteases, lipases) hydrolyze carbohydrates, proteins, and fats to nontoxic flavors and fragrances. Fermentation improves the sensory properties of a product and enriches it with beneficial microorganisms present in the gastrointestinal tract as well as with bioactive substances produced by these microorganisms. In addition, fermentation reduces the antinutritional substances in the product, such as phytates or protease inhibitors. Consequently, the contents of lysine, tryptophan, and vitamin B2 and the digestibility of the protein are increased. The increase in protein digestibility is due to the degradation of tannins and phytic acid by the enzymes produced by microorganisms during fermentation. An example of a fermented millet product is Saudi Arabian fermented bread known as lahoh. Although fermentation is a very effective method of millet processing, its use on a commercial scale is limited as this technology has so far been used only in home and laboratory conditions. Industrial use of this millet processing technology requires adapting the equipment and defining appropriate process conditions [2, 7].

In addition to the previously described millet processing methods, the grains can be prepared for consumption just by soaking it in water and subjecting it to thermal treatment. Soaking leads to a reduction in the content of antinutritive compounds, thereby increasing the bioavailability of the minerals present in the millet grains, such as iron and zinc [2].

Millet is a gluten-free cereal, and thus, millet-based products are ideal for consumers suffering from celiac disease or gluten intolerance. However, it is also a limiting factor from the technological perspective. Gluten is a plant protein that facilitates cereal products to absorb water and exhibit consistency, stickiness, and elasticity. Therefore, the lack of this protein in millet decreases its application in the baking industry, where it is usually combined with other cereals such as wheat as a result. However, millet can be used on a large scale for the production of plant-based beverages or breakfast cereals and groats [2, 8].

2.2 Characteristics and technology of millet beverage production

Millet beverages are consumed in the largest quantities in traditional forms such as fermented products. The fermentation process increases the nutritional value of the beverage, as well as ensuring its microbiological safety, without the need for additional preservatives. These types of products are a significant part of the diet mainly in India and African countries because they are identified as highly nutritious and safe food. For example, Jandh is one of the fermented millet beverages. It is a type of beer obtained by fermentation using lactic acid bacteria, yeast, and mold [9, 10].

The production of millet beverage without the fermentation process involves the procedures used in the production of most types of plant beverages. It also includes necessary elements based on the characteristics of the raw material. The stages involved in the production of millet beverage are shown in **Figure 1**. The millet beverage is usually obtained from whole millet grains or groats. When whole grains are used, they are properly prepared by soaking for a minimum period of 12 hours, followed by sprouting and drying. When using groats, the raw material is rinsed thoroughly to eliminate the bitter aftertaste [9, 11, 12].

The properly prepared raw material should be boiled until it reaches a thin consistency. After pretreatment, wet grinding is carried out. Soaking and water extraction allow preparing the raw material for further processing stages and facilitate the release of nutrients. Exposure to water leads to the inactivation of some inhibitors and a reduction in the amount of phytic acid, which consequently increases the absorption and bioavailability of nutrients. The obtained fluid is additionally heated to induce starch thermohydrolysis. At this stage, enzymes are also added to induce hydrolysis of starch. An example of an enzyme used is alpha-amylase, which hydrolyzes the α-1,4-glycosidic linkage of amylose and amylopectin in starch, resulting in shorter-chain compounds, mainly in the form of dextrins. The use of proteolytic enzymes increases protein digestibility and extraction efficiency, as well as improving the stability of the suspension [9, 12, 13].

The next step in the production of millet beverage is the separation of the solid fraction from the liquid fraction by filtration or centrifugation of the obtained

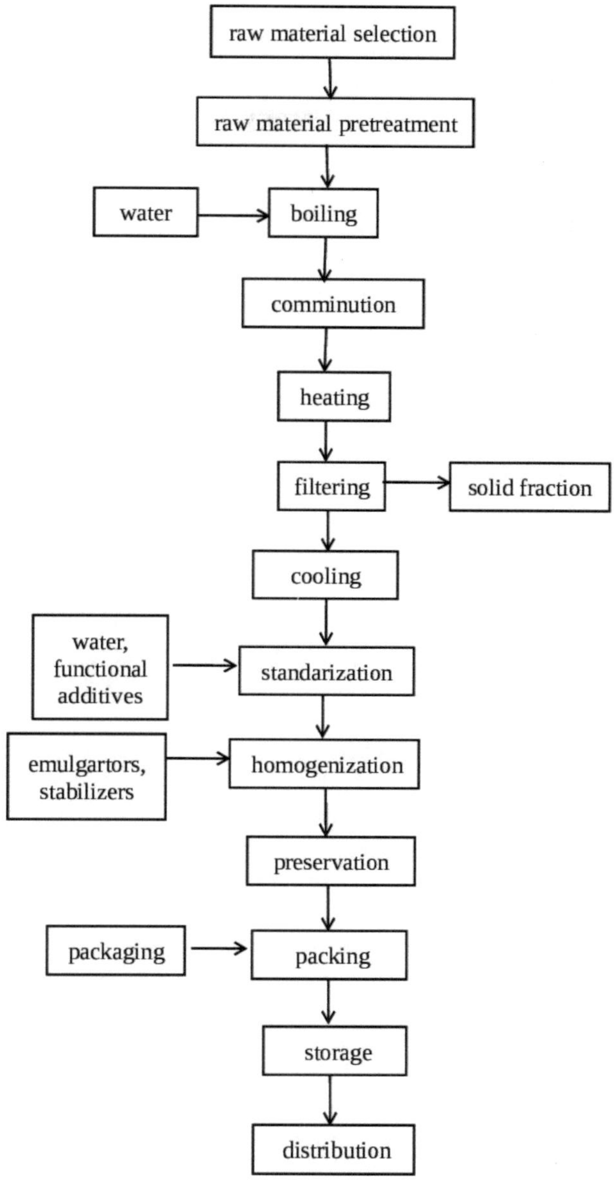

Figure 1.
Stages in the production of millet beverage [author's own study based on 9–11, 19].

suspension. As a result of the previous stages, the base of a plant beverage is obtained. The obtained base is subjected to the standardization process to obtain a product with the previously assumed composition. Standardization involves the addition of water, vegetable oils, vitamins, and minerals, as well as sweeteners, flavors, salts, and stabilizers. Vitamins and minerals are added to increase the nutritional value of the beverage and make it more similar to cow's milk. The fortifying substances selected for the beverage are required to be highly bioavailable and stable, and not cause excessive changes in the quality of the final product [9, 14, 15].

Millet beverages are characterized by low suspension stability due to the presence of solid particles, including protein, starch, fiber, and other residues of plant material. These particles have a higher density compared to water, and hence settle at the bottom of the beverage, making the product unstable. In order to increase the stability of millet beverages, homogenization process is carried out, which involves simultaneous grinding and mixing of the particles of the dispersed phase, while forcing the heterogeneous liquid system under high pressure (15–25 MPa) through the homogenizing gap. This operation is done to reduce the diameter and uniformity of the shape of the fat particles contained in the product. As a result, the obtained product is characterized by increased creaminess and homogeneity compared to nonhomogenized products. Homogenization is usually supported by the use of stabilizers, thickeners, and emulsifiers (e.g. cellulose, tapioca, carrageenan, pectin, locust bean gum, or lecithin), which increases the viscosity of the continuous phase, resulting in a uniform structure of the product [9, 15].

In order to ensure microbiological safety and extend the shelf life of plant beverages, thermal preservation methods are used, which mainly include pasteurization and ultrahigh temperature (UHT) treatment. Pasteurization is carried out at a temperature below 100°C, which results in a product with a shelf life of about 1 week at refrigerated temperatures. Such treatment destroys pathogenic microorganisms and inactivates the vegetative forms of other microorganisms. In UHT treatment, the product is heated in flow to 135–150°C for a few seconds to obtain a commercially sterile product. This process destroys the bacterial microflora, while maintaining the taste and aroma of the product. The obtained microbiologically safe product is poured into unit packages, stored, and finally distributed [9, 15].

2.3 Consumer acceptance of millet beverage in different forms

Consumers' acceptance of food products is influenced by many factors, including the characteristics of the offered product, consumer characteristics, and social conditions. Features of a food product such as its price, convenience, taste, general appearance, and health-promoting properties play an important role in its acceptance by consumers. Furthermore, consumer characteristics, such as the approach to innovation, preferences in relation to specific food groups, or nutritional neophobia determine the acceptance of food to a large extent. Food preferences vary among consumers of different age groups, in terms of knowledge about food, views on the health benefits of particular food groups, and attitudes toward food. Consumer acceptance is also influenced by social conditions, such as the country's economy, political conditions, or generally accepted social norms. Cultural factors and the origin of consumers are of great importance in the acceptance of a food product. Another important factor is the general public confidence in the food industry, as well as the existing differences in trust among consumers with regard to traditional and innovative food [16–18].

The consumer acceptance of millet beverage was assessed through a sensory analysis of the beverages produced in various types. The base of the millet beverage was obtained by combining 100 g of millet with 1000 g of tap water. The dry millet was first rinsed with hot water to eliminate the bitter aftertaste, and then added into boiling water and cooked covered for 40 minutes. After the set time, the obtained groats were combined with water, baled into a smooth slurry, and heated again for 5 minutes. The prepared suspension was sieved to obtain 1000 g of base millet beverage and 20 g of decoction. The base millet beverage was characterized by a high density, which was then subjected to two dilutions to prepare natural millet beverages: 1:2 (1 part base millet beverage was combined with 2 parts water) and 1:3 (1 part base millet beverage was combined with 3 parts water). Then, flavored millet beverages were prepared by combining with fruit purees (apple and banana), apple juice, and banana nectar. Thus, eight versions of millet beverages in three types were used as research material:

- millet beverage in a dilution of 1:2,
- millet beverage in a dilution of 1:3,
- base millet beverage in combination with apple juice,
- base millet beverage in combination with banana nectar,
- millet beverage in a 1:2 dilution in combination with apple puree,
- millet beverage in a 1:3 dilution in combination with apple puree,
- millet beverage in a 1:2 dilution in combination with banana puree,
- millet beverage in a 1:3 dilution in combination with banana puree.

The sensory analysis of the obtained millet beverages was conducted using an original questionnaire prepared for sensory evaluation. The evaluation was performed by a group of 15 students of Dietetics, Faculty of Human Nutrition, Warsaw University of Life Sciences (SGGW—WULS), who had previously declared their will to consume plant-based beverages. The beverages were prepared 4 days in advance and were cooled in a refrigerator at 8 degrees Celsius until evaluation. The chilled beverages were served as 30 ml samples in coded disposable cups with a volume of 200 cm3, in a random order for sensory evaluation. The Statistica 13.1 program was used for statistical analysis of the results. The statistical methods used were analysis of variance—simple ANOVA sections and post hoc analysis—LSD test (last significant differences) [19].

During the sensory evaluation of the tested millet beverages of various types, their taste, smell, color, and consistency were tested. Each of the features was assessed on a 5-point scale, where rating 5 meant that the beverage was very favorable whereas 1 meant that the beverage was very unfavorable. The millet beverage in combination with apple juice (average rating 4.33), millet beverage in a dilution of 1:2 in combination with banana puree (average rating 4.53), and millet beverage in a dilution of 1:3 in combination with banana puree (average rating 4.33) were rated the most favorable in terms of taste. The natural millet beverage in a dilution of 1:2 was rated the least favorable in terms of taste. In terms of color, all the tested beverages were rated at a similar level, and the average ratings were between 3 and 4. Millet beverages in both dilutions in combination with banana puree were rated as the most favorable flavored beverages (average rating 4.60). The millet beverages in the natural form in the dilutions of 1:2 (average rating 2.53) and 1:3 (average rating 2.73) were rated as the least favorable in terms of aroma. The millet beverage in combination with apple juice (average rating of 3.80), the millet beverage in a dilution of 1:2 in combination with banana puree (average rating of 3.80), and the millet beverage in a dilution of 1:3 in combination with banana puree (average rating 3.87) were rated as the most favorable in terms of consistency. The results of the analysis of variance for the mean values given for the sensory traits of the assessed millet beverages of different types are presented as a sensory profile graph in **Figure 2** [19].

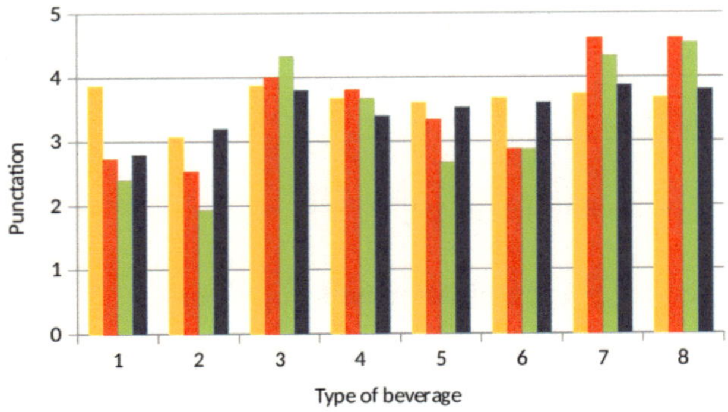

Figure 2.
Sensory profiles of the evaluated millet beverages of different types [19]. Legend: Color. Smell. Taste. Consistency.*1 - millet beverage in a dilution of 1:2, 2 - millet beverage in a dilution of 1:3, 3 - base millet beverage in combination with apple juice, 4 - base millet beverage in combination with banana nectar, 5 - millet beverage in a 1:2 dilution in combination with apple puree, 6 - millet beverage in a 1:3 dilution in combination with apple puree, 7 - millet beverage in a 1:2 dilution in combination with banana puree, 8 - millet beverage in a 1:3 dilution in combination with banana puree.*

The LSD test was used to compare the results obtained from the sensory evaluation of the tested millet beverages in pairs and to evaluate the statistical significance of the calculated differences. The tested pairs were as follows:

- natural millet beverage in a 1:2 dilution and natural millet beverage in a 1:3 dilution,
- millet beverage in combination with apple juice and millet beverage in combination with banana nectar,
- millet beverage in a 1:2 dilution with apple puree and millet beverage in a 1:3 dilution with apple puree, and
- millet beverage in a 1:2 dilution with banana puree and millet beverage in a 1:3 dilution with banana puree.

In terms of taste, no significant differences were found between natural millet beverages in both dilutions, millet beverages in combination with apple puree in both dilutions, and millet beverages in combination with banana puree in both dilutions. The millet beverage in combination with apple juice was assessed to be significantly better than the millet beverage in combination with banana nectar. The results of the LSD test for the trait "taste" of the evaluated millet beverages are presented in **Figure 3** [19].

In terms of color, significant differences were found only in the case of natural millet beverages. The natural millet beverage in a 1:3 dilution was assessed to be significantly better than the natural millet beverage in a 1:2 dilution. No statistically significant differences were found between the remaining pairs of millet beverages. The results of the LSD test for the trait "color" of the assessed millet beverages are presented in **Figure 4** [19].

In terms of smell, no statistically significant differences were found between the compared pairs of beverages. The results of the LSD test for the trait "smell" of the assessed millet beverages are presented in **Figure 5** [19].

In terms of consistency, no statistically significant differences were found between the compared pairs of beverages. The results of the LSD test for the trait "consistency" of the evaluated millet beverages are presented in **Figure 6** [19].

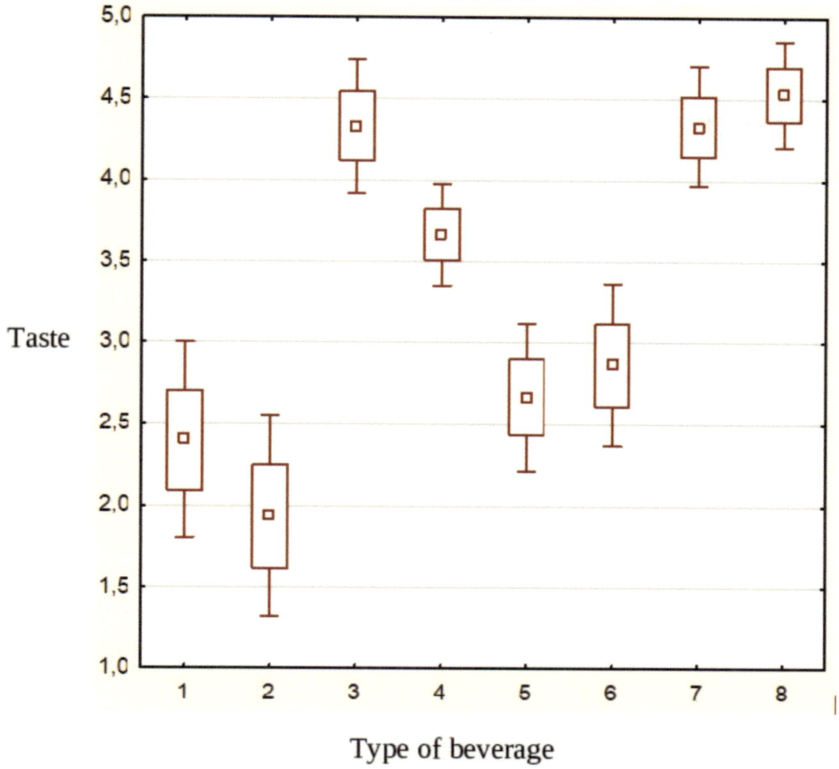

Figure 3.
Categorized box–whisker chart for trait TASTE of the rated millet beverages [19]. The legend is the same as for ***Figure 2****.*

In the conducted research, taste, smell, color, and consistency were considered as some of the main characteristics that guide consumers in the purchase of food products [20].

According to people who performed the sensory evaluation, the millet beverages with apple and banana flavors were the best in terms of taste. Banana nectars and purees are characterized by a high intensity of taste and sweetness, which could have influenced the sensory assessors to positively evaluate the beverages containing them. The evaluators rated the natural millet beverage in a dilution of 1:2 as the poorest in terms of taste. Such an assessment could have resulted from the plant aftertaste of the beverages in its natural form, which may not be accepted by all consumers, and also from its high turbidity caused by low dilution [19].

The color ratings of all the tested millet beverages remained at a similar level. Each type of beverage had a specific color, which may have prompted the evaluators to give similar ratings. The only significant difference in terms of color ratings was found between the natural millet beverages. The natural millet beverage in a 1:3 dilution was rated better than that in a 1:2 dilution. Higher dilution gave the beverage a less "milky" color, which is more similar to the color of plant-based beverages available on the market and could be the reason for the higher ratings obtained by the high-diluted natural millet beverage [19].

The smell of the natural millet beverage turned out to be the least favorable to the evaluators and was rated the lowest. The banana puree masked the "millet" smell to the greatest extent, which, when combined with the millet beverage, gave it a specific smell. The beverages in combination with banana purees, in both dilutions, therefore turned out to be the most advantageous in terms of aroma for the evaluators and hence were rated the highest [19].

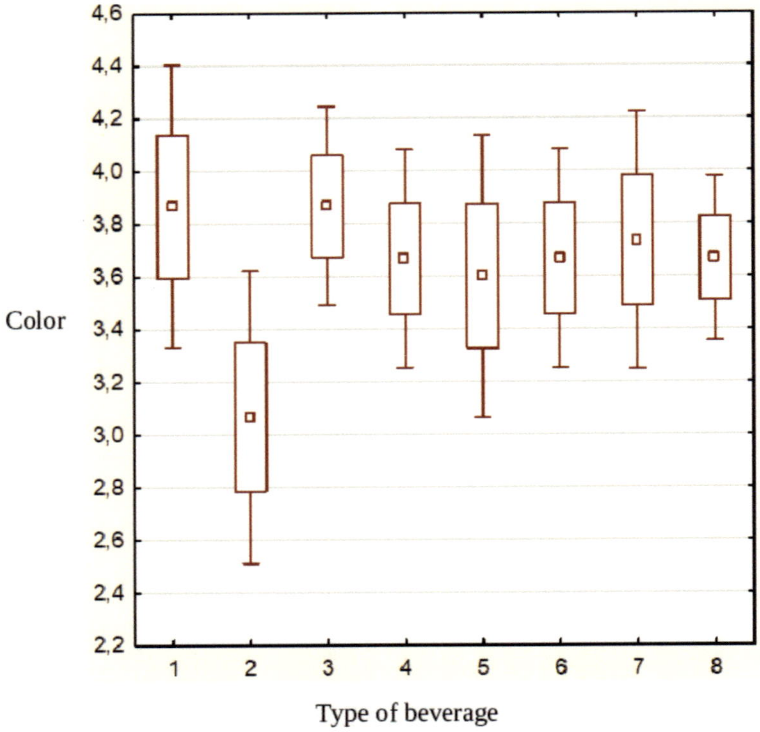

Figure 4.
Categorized box–whisker chart for trait COLOR of the rated millet beverages [19]. The legend is the same as for ***Figure*** 2.

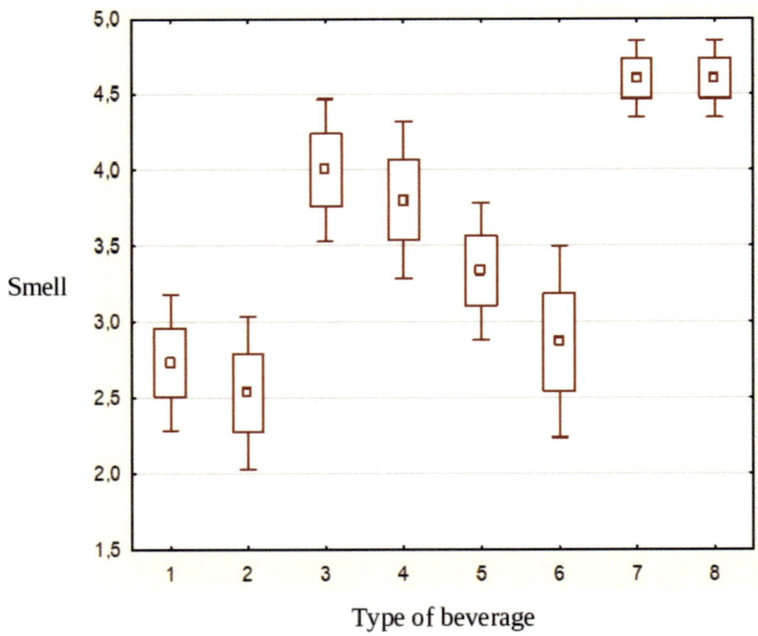

Figure 5.
Categorized box–whisker chart for trait SMELL of the rated millet beverages [19]. The legend is the same as for ***Figure*** 2.

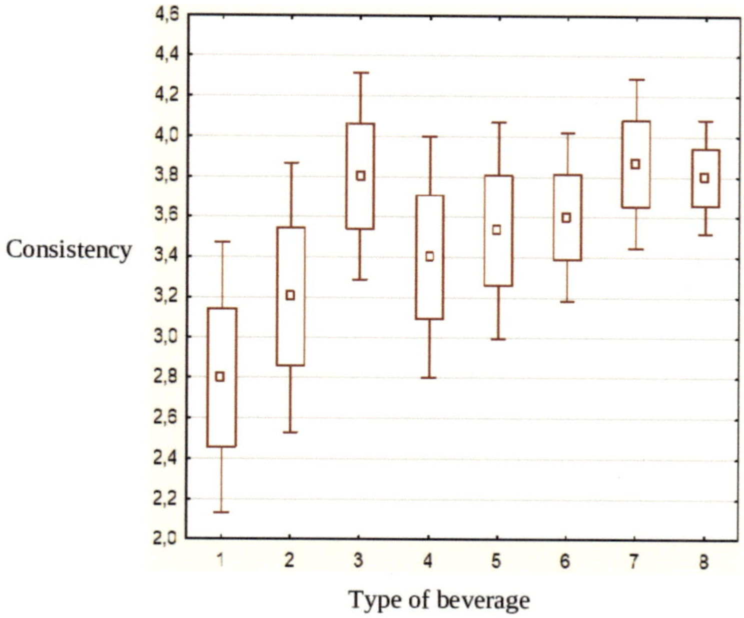

Figure 6.
*Categorized box–whisker chart for trait CONSISTENCY of the rated millet beverages [19]. The legend is the same as for **Figure 2**.*

The most favorable results in terms of consistency were observed for the millet beverage in combination with apple juice and the millet beverage in combination with banana purees, in both dilutions. Millet beverage in combination with apple juice and millet beverage in a dilution of 1:3 in combination with banana puree showed a similar consistency, specific to refreshing beverages. High ratings given for these types of beverages indicate the consumers' interest in such alternatives available on the market. Millet beverage in a 1:2 dilution in combination with a banana puree with a smoothie consistency was also given high ratings [19].

3. Conclusions

Owing to the increase in the popularity of the plant-based diet and thus increasing interest in plant-based beverages, there is a need to develop new products in this category and improve the existing ones.

Millet and millet products are characterized by high nutritional value and technological suitability and can therefore be included in the daily diet.

The structure of millet beverages is suitable for their use in the form of both refreshing beverages (with more water) and smoothies (with less water).

Natural millet beverages have low consumer acceptance. However, the addition of fruit juices and purees during their production can contribute to increasing their sensory attractiveness.

Conflict of interest

Authors have declared that they do not have any conflict of interest for publishing this research.

Author details

Patrycja Cichońska* and Małgorzata Ziarno
Division of Milk Technology, Department of Food Technology and Assessment, Institute of Food Science, Warsaw University of Life Sciences - SGGW (WULS-SGGW), Warsaw, Poland

*Address all correspondence to: cichonskapatrycja@gmail.com

References

[1] Amadou I, Gounga M, Le GW. Millets: Nutritional composition, some health benefits and processing – A Review. Emirates Journal of Food and Agriculture. 2013;25(7):501-508. DOI: 10.9755/ejfa.v25i7.12045

[2] Saleh A, Zhang Q, Chen J, Shen Q. Millet Grains: Nutritional Quality, Processing, and Potential Health Benefits. Comprehensive Reviews in Food Science and Food Safety. 2013:12(3):281-295. DOI:10.1111/1541-4337.12012

[3] Świetlikowska K. Rośliny zbożowe. In: Janda E, editors. Surowce spożywcze pochodzenia roślinnego. Warsaw; 2008. p. 206-242. ISBN: ISBN: 978-83-7244-929-0 (in Polish)

[4] Kunachowicz H, Przygoda B, Nadolna I, Iwanow K, editors. Tabele składu i wartości odżywczej żywności. 2nd ed. Warsaw 2019. ISBN: 9788320053111 (in Polish)

[5] Waszkiewicz-Robak B. Technologia oraz ocena jakości przetworów zbożowych: mąk, kasz, makaronów. In: Świderski F, Waszkiewicz-Robak B, editors. Towaroznawstwo Żywności Przetworzonej z Elementami Technologii. Warsaw; 2010. p. 374-404. ISBN: 978-83-7583-210-5 (in Polish)

[6] Lebiedzińska A, Szefer P. Vitamins B in grain and cereal–grain food, soy-products and seeds. Food Chemistry. 2006;1:116-122. DOI: 10.1016/j.foodchem.2004.12.024

[7] Trząskowska M. Probiotics in Products of Plant Origin. Food : Science - Technology - Quality. 2013;4(89):5-20. DOI: 10.15193/zntj/2013/89/005-020 (in Polish, Abstract in English)

[8] Wieser H. Chemistry of gluten proteins. Food Microbiology. 2007;24(2):115-119. DOI: 10.1016/j.fm.2006.07.004

[9] Mäkinen OE, Wanhalinna V, Zannini E, Arendt EK. Foods for special dietary needs: Non-dairy plant based milk substitutes and fermented dairy type products. Critical Reviews in Food Science and Nutrition, 2015;56(3):339-49. DOI: 10.1080/10408398.2012.761950

[10] Amadou I, Gbadamosi OS, Le GW. Millet-based Traditional Processed Foods and Beverages—A Review. Cereal Foods World. 2011;56(3):115-121. DOI: 10.1094/CFW-56-3-0115

[11] Kumar A, Kaur A, Tomer v, Rasane P, Gupta K. Development of nutricereals and milk-based beverage: Process optimization and validation of improved nutritional properties. Journal of Food Process Engineering. 2019;43:e13025. DOI: 10.1111/jfpe.13025

[12] Shunmugapriya K, Kanchana S, Maheswari TU, Kumar RS, Vanniarajan C. Standardization and Stabilization of Millet Milk by Enzyme and Its Physicochemical Evaluation. European Journal of Nutrition & Food Safety. 2020;12(1):30-38. DOI: 10.9734/EJNFS/2020/v12i130181

[13] Gupta R, Gangoliya S, Singh N. Reduction of phytic acid and enhancement of bioavailable micronutrients in food grains. Journal of Food Science and Technology. 2015;52(2):676-682. DOI: 10.1007/s13197-013-0978-y

[14] Pilarska AA, Gawałek J. Hydrocolloids as stabilizers used in food industry, functions in food. Part I. Modifications and applicable laws. Przemysł Spożywczy. 2016;70(3):36-39. DOI: 10.15199/65.2016.3.5 (in Polish, Abstract in English)

[15] Swati S, Tyagi SK, Anurag RK. Plant-based milk alternatives an emerging segment of functional beverages: a review. Journal of

Food Science and Technology. 2016;53(9):3408-3423. DOI: 10.1007/ s13197-016-2328-3

[16] Jeżewska-Zychowicz M. Determinants of Consumer Acceptance of Innovative Food Products. Food: Science - Technology - Quality. 2014;6(97):5-17. DOI: 10.15193/ ZNTJ/2014/97/005-017 (in Polish, Abstract in English)

[17] Siegrist M, Shi J, Giusto A, Hartmann C. Worlds apart. Consumer acceptance of functional foods and beverages in Germany and China. Appetite. 2015;92(1):87-93. DOI: 10.1016/j.appet.2015.05.017

[18] Sajdakowska M, Jankowski P, Gutkowska K, Guzek D, Żakowska-Biermans S, Ozimek I. Consumer acceptance of innovations in food: A survey among Polish consumers. Journal of Consumer Behaviour. 2018;17(3): 253-267. DOI: 10.1002/cb.1708

[19] Cichońska P. [thesis]. The research on consumer preferences regarding the consumption of cereal beverages and developing the recipe for a millet beverage. Warsaw University of Life Sciences; 2018. (in Polish, Abstract in English)

[20] Niewczas M. Food Choice Criteria. Food : Science - Technology – Quality. 2013;6(91):204-219. DOI: 10.15193/ zntj/2013/91/204-219 (in Polish, Abstract in English)

Section 2

Technology and Application of Milk Substitutes in Human and Animal Nutrition

Chapter 3

Stability Aspects of Non-Dairy Milk Alternatives

Jyotika Dhankhar and Preeti Kundu

Abstract

In recent years, plant-based milk products, commonly called as non-dairy milk alternatives have gained high popularity due to concerns associated with bovine milk like lactose intolerance, allergies, hypercholesterolemia, and pesticide and antibiotic residues. Important strategies for manufacture of non-dairy milk alternatives involve disintegration of plant materials in aqueous medium; its homogenization and addition of some additives to attain a consistency and appearance similar to that of bovine milk. Different range of ingredients are added to non-dairy milk alternatives such as oils, emulsifiers, thickeners, antioxidants, minerals etc. The main problem associated with non-dairy milk alternatives is generally linked with its stability. Stability is a crucial factor that governs the sensory properties and overall acceptance of non-dairy milk alternatives. Differences in processing parameters and molecular interaction mechanisms affect the stability of emulsions as well as the stability of non-dairy milk manufactured thereof. Various treatments like thermal treatment, non-thermal processing (ultra high pressure homogenization, pulsed electric field, ultrasonication), addition of emulsifiers are effective in achieving the stability of non-dairy milks. The present chapter aims to summarize the various factors contributing to the physical stability of non-dairy milk alternatives like appearance, consistency, emulsion stability, and the approaches required to maintain it.

Keywords: non-dairy milk alternatives, emulsifiers, thickeners, ultra high pressure homogenization, stability

1. Introduction

Food has served multitude of functions for humans since ages, such as satiating hunger, quenching the palate with different savory food products, promoting well-being and socializing on one side of the equation, and providing the basis of energy production for regulating physiological needs, acting as a source of health promoting bioactive components, and antioxidants, on other. Among the foods, animal based products like bovine milk and beef are by far the most commonly consumed ones in the world. Apart from reasons of health and wellbeing, consumers nowadays are interested in reducing their intake of animal products because of moral and environmental reasons. Different issues underlying the negative attitude towards the manufacture of animal based products include environmental pressures from the vast amounts of agricultural produce and water essential for feeding animals, habitat loss deforestation, animal exploitation, species extinction, and pollution in production and transportation of the food until it reaches the consumer.

Since in recent years the animal based diet is being negatively associated with the individual's health and the environment, people have started looking for other food options [1]. Consequently, the plant based diet has become a favorite among people because of its potential to promote health, to improve food security, and to decrease pollution, land use, and water use [2].

Because of the increase in the global urban population, and with the consumers having more purchasing power and health awareness nowadays, the demand for healthier, tastier, and newer food products has risen tremendously. Furthermore, research for various innovative and novel food product developments in the last decade has been focused on meeting the emerging needs and adapting to existing market demands by providing newer food choices and alternatives. Therefore, the plant based diets like non-dairy milk alternatives, in particular, seem to have experienced a surge in the market. Besides, there is increasing negative perception related to the consumption of bovine milk among consumers as it has been linked adversely to many diseases such as bovine milk allergy, lactose intolerance, anemia, and coronary heart diseases for the past many years [3–5] and also due to issues that have raised concern in recent years, like the presence of toxic chemicals, antibiotics, contaminants, and greenhouse gas emissions. Nondairy milk alternatives possess health beneficial components, including antioxidant, antimicrobial, dietary fibers, unsaturated fatty acids; and hence, are desirable among consumers [6–8]. Nonetheless, the market for non-dairy milk alternatives is still emerging and currently, the range of products available in the market include hazelnut, peanut, sesame, soy, almond, oat, rice, hemp, and walnut milk; issues regarding the stability and nutritional value is still a concern among consumers. For successful commercialization of non-dairy milk alternatives, processors are often interested in the technological interventions and ingredients that can help maintain the physical stability of the final product. Physical stability refers to the maintenance of inherent attributes of suspension in relation to its viscosity, appearance, consistency, color, and resistance to destabilization mechanisms like sedimentation, phase separation, flocculation, creaming, etc. The general manufacturing process involves soaking the raw material (nut, legume, cereals, pseudocereal) in water, disintegrating moist material, separating oil bodies, adding different additives, heating for killing the harmful microorganisms, homogenization, and aseptic packaging [9]. Technological interventions are required to manufacture milk substitutes equivalent to bovine milk in their appearance, flavor, stability, and nutritional components. Most of these milks are unstable during manufacturing and storage; they tend to undergo phase separation and spoilage on long term storage. For these reasons, various methods have been employed to achieve stability in these non-dairy milks, for instance, by incorporation of different types of additives, such as gums, thickeners, emulsifiers, and by application of new technologies, like ultra-high-pressure homogenization, ultrasound, and pulsed electric fields. Therefore, while formulating non-dairy milk alternatives, it is necessary to endeavor towards utilizing the beneficial properties of plant materials and employing appropriate technologies for manufacturing non-dairy milks such that they are stable, display functional characteristics and sensory attributes similar to those of bovine milk. The aim of this chapter is to discuss the processing steps, mechanisms underlying the physical instability and to explore possible solutions with regard to use of different additives and advanced technological interventions in manufacture of non-dairy milks.

2. Need for stability of non-dairy milk alternatives

Bovine milk is nature's most complete food [10] with different components present in heterogeneous mixture like carbohydrates, whey proteins and minerals in solution; fat globules in emulsion while casein micelles and some minerals are distributed in colloidal phase, giving the bovine milk its typical composition and structure [11]. Being a rich source of nutrients, bovine milk is a perishable food item and is often subjected to heat treatments, like pasteurization to extend shelf life for a week on refrigeration; UHT for shelf life extension to several months at ambient temperature [12]. In general, different processing operations, like heat treatment and homogenization are greatly influenced by the structural design of bovine milk components conferring it suitability for use in different food systems [13]. However, in case of the plant-based milk alternatives, sales trend suggest that the customers are hesitant to buy them because they display undesirable behavior when served hot or on blending with the hot drinks.

Therefore, the beneficial qualities of the bovine milk must be closely reproduced by plant based milks, if they are to be perceived better than or equal to them. During the formulation of plant-based milk substitutes, it is essential to adopt effective technologies and suitable ingredients to achieve the stability to overcome the problems of unacceptable flavor and phase separation on storage, commonly associated with the beverages. Different novel technologies that have been applied for achieving stabilization involve reduction in particle size, decrease in viscosity, and decrease in microbial count [14–19].

It has been demonstrated that size of dispersed phase particles in plant-based milks is one of the important factors governing their stability [15, 20, 21]. Plant-based milks are colloidal dispersions consisting of wide range of components such as fat globules, ground raw material, proteins and carbohydrates etc. They often contribute to unstable product on storage as they tend to exhibit phenomena like creaming, sedimentation and phase separation. Besides, non-dairy milks are often associated with sandy, gritty or chalky mouthfeel and tend to develop off flavors during storage [22, 23]. Also, during formulation of non-dairy milk substitutes, bovine milk fat globule is an ideal candidate that needs to be simulated due to its significant contribution to the creaminess, texture and flavor of dairy products. To develop non-dairy milk alternatives, fat phase is incorporated either through addition of oil bodies [24] or fabrication of fat globules from plant sources [25].

It is essential to take different aspects in account, such as kind of raw material, shelf stability, processing operations and various electrostatic interactions underlying phase destabilization (creaming, flocculation, sedimentation, coalescence) while manufacturing non-dairy milks. With regard to stability of non-dairy milk alternatives, one fundamental attribute that is relevant to most of the products is their colloidal nature since other features like composition, and structure often vary markedly among different brands. Therefore, different characteristics that need to be monitored accurately in non-dairy milks, include properties of colloidal particles such as their size, charge density, surface charge, and surface properties, the nature of the continuous aqueous phase (the pH, ionic concentration, components, density, and viscosity), and the extent of exposure to external environment during its shelf life (storage temperature and time). Plant based milks not only undergo objectionable changes in physicochemical properties but also show signs of microbial spoilage on long term storage. Some of the necessary ingredients, processing techniques, and phenomena governing the physical stability of plant-based milks during manufacture and storage have been discussed below.

3. Processing steps for manufacturing non-dairy milk alternatives

During the manufacture of non-dairy milk alternatives, they are often subjected to various preprocessing treatments like dehulling, soaking, sprouting, blanching etc., to assist in subsequent processing. In general, the processing of milk from plants involves two main methods, namely, wet and dry. Otherwise, product is formulated by reconstitution using protein isolates or concentrates, water and other ingredients like oils, sugars, salts and stabilizers [26]. In the wet process, plant based raw material is soaked and ground with the water into a slurry, while in the dry method, the plant based material is ground into flour and then extracted with water. Such material is then subjected to filtration to remove insoluble or coarse particles to obtain aqueous phase. Afterwards, the processing steps followed include the addition of ingredients like oil, sugar, salts, colors, flavors, and stabilizers; homogenization and thermal processing treatments to yield non-dairy milk alternatives with desirable attributes.

3.1 Preliminary processing treatments

3.1.1 Dehulling

Dehulling operation involves the mechanical breaking of thick and hard seed coats of plant based raw materials before soaking to facilitate hydration. The strength of binding of the hull to endosperm governs the time required for dehulling procedure. Since the hull has a hydrophobic nature due to its association with hemicellulose and pentosans, it tends to lower down the hydration capacity of plant material. The polysaccharides present in the hull often lead to off-flavor, and foaming during processing, hence, their removal improves the processing operation and organoleptic properties of product. Also, microorganisms and enzymic activity associated with hulls reduces on dehulling. The traditional method includes initially exposing the raw material to the sun for drying and then dehulling with mortar and pestle. Alternatively, they are dehulled using the mills, and may also be milled using splitting machine, which employs both splitting and dehulling simultaneously. The milk prepared from dehulled raw material allows for production of a shelf stable and appealing final product.

3.1.2 Roasting

Roasting is a thermal process encompassing dehydration of raw material [27] for its improved flavor, aroma, and milling properties. Decrease in protein, starch content and improved extraction yield of roasted pulses and grains have been reported by many authors [28, 29]. Studies have shown that roasting leads to improved protein digestibility, and reduction in antinutritional compounds found in raw pulses and nuts. The decrease in protein content has been ascribed to the partial loss of amino acids, as well as of some nitrogenous compounds, and the reduction in starch to the solubilization of starch during the thermal process. Also, roasting has been shown to increase the water absorption capacity and water absorption index. An increase in WAC and WAI is related to the denaturation of proteins and starch gelatinization, which contribute to enhanced water imbibition [30]. Therefore, the flours with higher WAC are likely to result in the more viscous non-dairy alternative compared to untreated ones. Thermal processing during roasting results in partial disruption of the raw material [31, 32], thereby facilitating efficient particle size reduction required for stable suspension of non-dairy milk alternatives. For manufacturing milk from nuts and seeds, which contain high levels of unsaturated fatty acids, roasting should be carried out in controlled conditions of time and temperature to improve their nutritional properties and for prevention of off flavor development due to oxidation of unsaturated fatty acids. Inactivation of lipoxygenase during the process improves the flavor of non-dairy alternatives like soy milk, peanut milk, melon milk, sesame milk [33–37]. Roasted plant material becomes drier and brittle, and the non-dairy alternatives obtained from them are likely less-creamy [36]. In the study for manufacture of sesame milk, it was studied that the roasting process decreased acidity, total solids content and improved sensory profile by decreasing bitterness and a chalky taste associated with the milk [37]. The product obtained upon roasting has improved nutritional and sensory properties.

3.1.3 Sprouting

Sprouting refers to the soaking of seeds in water for specified time (1–14 hours) depending on the kind (variety, size, shape) of food grains in order to hydrate them for breaking their dormancy. The soaked grains are subsequently drained and rinsed at regular intervals to enable sprouting. Sprouting results in the initiation of series of metabolic changes in seeds (legumes, cereals, nuts & oilseeds) that improves the nutritional quality by inactivating the anti-nutritional factors such as trypsin inhibitor and phytic acid [38]. The improvement in nutritional value occurs due to enhanced activities of hydrolytic enzymes, which cause the conversion of stored chemical compounds, such as protein, starch and lipids into simple compounds; thereby, increasing the levels of total proteins, fat, certain essential amino acids, total sugars, B-group vitamins and decreasing the levels of starch. Therefore, the sprouting of raw material assists in the development of non-dairy milk alternatives, which are generally prepared using the heat treatment to decrease anti nutrient factors. Because sprouting is a natural biochemical process involving enzymatic activity, the treatment yields the improved quality of final product in terms of the nutrient and sensory value. Such a treatment decreases the intensity of heat treatment required for the manufacture of the product. Sprouting ensues improved protein solubility and reduced fat content for raw materials, which decreases the viscosity of non-dairy milk alternatives [38, 39]. Also, improvement in sensory properties takes place due to absence of beany flavor.

3.1.4 Blanching

Blanching with hot water is employed to inactivate enzymes like lipoxygenase and trypsin inhibitors for improvement of the flavor and nutritional value of the non-dairy milk alternatives [40]. Such a treatment has been reported to be effective in diminishing the beany, grassy, bitter, and rancid flavor; it also prevents suspension instability and chalkiness in non-dairy milks prepared from peanuts, soybean, almonds etc. [41–45]. Blanching with hot water (85–100 °C for 2–5 min) is commonly used for skin removal of raw materials and overcoming off flavors in non-dairy milk alternatives. Like roasting, blanching inactivates enzymes, reduces possible microbial contamination, and aids in deskinning in processing by wet or dry methods [46]. Pressure blanching (at 121 °C, 15 psi for 3 min) has been found to be effective for developing peanut milk with desirable sensory and physicochemical properties [47]. The treatment yields the milk with pleasing sensory attributes because blanching treatment for suitable time decreases the total solids and nutty flavor associated with peanut milk. The treated milk has improved consistency as well as decreased soaking time.

3.2 Wet processing

3.2.1 Soaking

The process for manufacturing of non-dairy milk alternatives involves the soaking of raw material in the proper volume of water contained in large stainless steel containers. Soaking is done to hydrate the raw material (cereals, legumes, nuts, or seeds) for grinding and further processing. Time required for soaking depends on the nature of raw material and temperature of the soaking water. At an ambient temperature, soaking requires longer time, and souring may take place due to bacterial growth, whereas if the temperature is raised up to 50–80 °C, soaking time is decreased, and hydration is accelerated. It has been demonstrated that during the soaking of lentils at different temperatures (20, 50, and 80 °C), rate of hydration at 50 and 80 °C was four to six fold higher than at 20 °C [48]. Softening due to soaking at higher temperatures could be related to the heat-induced modification in biomolecules, including starch, pectin, and protein, and the moisture for making the biomolecules susceptible to the changes. Different processes for preparation of non-dairy milks like peanut, soy, almond milk include soaking the raw material for 12 to 18 h before grinding it either in the mixer grinder or in colloidal mill [45]. Soaking facilitates the inactivation of enzyme inhibitors, improves digestibility and bioavailability of nutrients [49]. In case of pulses and grains, soaking step reduces the polyphenols and eliminates the alkaloids (e.g., in lupin) present in some of them; decreases the cooking time; improves the protein bioavailability and assists in peeling or dehulling [50, 51]. Soaking in acidic or basic solution is done to facilitate peeling of walnuts, almonds, tiger nuts, Brazilian nuts etc. Studies have shown that basic solution (1–2% NaOH) is suitable for peeling of walnuts and Brazil nuts [52–53] while citric acid is effective for peeling tiger nuts [54].

3.2.2 Wet milling or grinding

The procedure involves the grinding or milling of the plant material with the use of water for the split opening of the exterior hull. Wet grinding consists of grinding of fresh raw materials with the water to result in a suspension. The wet grinding method tends to produce finer particle size of the ground material [55] that results in more stability of non-dairy milk alternatives, and therefore, is more commonly used for their manufacture. In general, a colloid mill is used for reducing the particle size of raw material in suspension. Initially, the coarse grinding of raw material is done, which is followed by fine grinding. During the wet milling with the colloid mill, the rotor generates a substantial amount of stress by the rotation of the rotary stirrer, which can effectively accomplish the creation of submicron particles. In addition to disintegration, the colloid milling performs broad spectrum of functions like mixing, blending, and homogenizing effects [56]. In the manufacturing of the non-dairy milk alternative, this technique is mostly used for homogenization and emulsification [57]. The optimization of colloidal milling process parameters improves the physical stability of non-dairy milk alternatives by efficiently reducing the size of dispersed particles [58]. Different studies have shown that the amount of water added for wet milling depends on the kind of raw material, for instance, almond milk (1:9; almond& water), Sesame (1:5; sesame & water), Peanut (1:9; Peanut: water), soybean (1:5; soy: water) [15, 36, 37, 59]. Wet milling contributes the formulation of stable product where different factors like rotor speed, temperature, ratio of raw material and water can be fine-tuned to achieve any kind of non-dairy milk alternative.

3.3 Dry processing

The dry process comprises drying the raw materials and milling them into flours. For improving the efficiency of dry grinding, the raw material should be dried to minimum water content. The flour may be subsequently treated to yield different fractions: the protein, the starch and fiber. The protein concentrate or isolate, afterwards, is often utilized in formulation of non-dairy beverage. Therefore, dry processing mostly leads to development of product with higher protein contents.

3.3.1 Dry milling or grinding

The dry milling is mostly employed to reduce the particle size of the dried raw materials into their respective powder forms. The ground material is then mixed with water to form paste. However, during the manufacturing of the non-dairy alternative from pastes, solids tend to settle out down in the container, thereby resulting in the incomplete transfer of the content to the homogenizer and its wastage as well. For ensuring the efficient fuctioning of the dry grinding process, the important factors to be considered are the particle stiffness and feed size. Although the dry grinding decreases water wastage and energy consumption, yields a product with higher quality of protein, carbohydrates, fat, and minerals, it is less popular due to handling problems, like dust and wastage of raw material.

3.4 Extraction

For manufacturing the non-dairy milk alternative, the raw material, once it has been subjected to preliminary processing treatments, is extracted with water. The extraction efficiency can be improved by variation of pH or enzymatic treatment.

3.4.1 Extraction by variation of pH

The pH during extraction dictates the efficiency of protein extraction and stability of emulsion in non-dairy milk. Globulins comprise a major fraction of plant proteins, while albumins represent a minor fraction [60–62]. The pI for globulins is near pH 4.5, whereas the pI of albumins is around pH 6. The pI for different plant proteins lies between these values. Different studies have also demonstrated that plant proteins like pea, lentil, chickpea, soy etc. have a low net charge around pH 5 [63]. The plant proteins are mostly stable to pH changes at all pH values except at pH 5, which is around the pI where the droplets carry no charge and tend to display phase destabilization phenomena like aggregation and flocculation. During extraction, proteins should a have a high net charge at pH values well above or below their isoelectric point, which solubilizes them to increase the yield. Extraction in alkaline pH exhibits improved protein extraction yield, which may then be followed by neutralization step. For achieving the higher yield of the process, the efficiency of this step may be improved by alkalization of the medium using bicarbonate or NaOH.

3.4.2 Extraction using enzymatic treatment

Enzymatic treatment for hydrolysis of proteins and polysaccharides is mostly employed to improve the extraction yields. Disruption of plant cell wall components like cellulose, hemicelluloses, and pectin is facilitated by enzymes to improve the yield. The efficiency of protein and oil extraction is closely related with cell wall disruption of plant based material [64]. Studies have shown that cell wall degrading enzymes with pectinolytic activity like polygalacturonase, pectate lyaese, or pectin methyl esterase enhance the extractability of protein, fat, and antioxidant activity [65–67]. Also, upon application of cell wall degrading enzymes (cellulase, hemicellulase, pectinase) after homogenization step helps reduce the particle size, thereby facilitating suspension stability [68]. Because of the reduced particle size of suspended material, the enzyme treated non-dairy milks exhibit improved physical stability and flavor. Rosenthal et al. [68] reported that enzymatic treatment (1.2% of Celluclast) decreased the tendency of soymilk to undergo sedimentation on storage and improved sensorial attributes in terms of improved viscosity and lack of chalkiness. Proteolytic enzymes tend to improve the extraction yield and suspension stability [69]. A high solubility is required for the proteins because it governs their functional properties, for instance, emulsification, which subsequently affects the colloidal stability of the emulsion. The extraction of protein also increases due to improved solubility of proteins. Other enzymatic treatments involving the use of carbohydrate degrading enzymes like amyloglucosidase, amylases etc. have been demonstrated to improve the carbohydrate recovery and stability of non-dairy milk alternatives. Depending upon the plant based material containing appreciable amount of starch, for instance, in case of cereals & pseudocereals, liquefaction with α-and β-amylases is done for starch hydrolysis [70–72]. Upon heating, starch gelatinizes to set as thick gel during heating, and hence enzymatic treatment is required to maintain the non-dairy milk in the liquid state. The liquefaction treatment increases the yield due to hydrolysis of starch into maltodextrin, thereby improving the viscosity for the non-dairy milk alternative. Since it facilitates the filtration, the enzyme treatment is often employed during or before filtration; however, it might also be used after filtration, subject to the conditions. Studies have shown that starch liquefaction using amylases generally improves the viscosity and overall acceptability in non-dairy milk alternatives like oat milk, quinoa milk, rice milk, [72–74].

3.5 Filtration

Following the extraction step, removal of okara (the water-insoluble portion) from the slurry is done to obtain aqueous portion for manufacturing non-dairy milk alternative. The separation step is achieved by employing either batch process using filter cloth or continuous process like centrifugation [75, 76]. In general, two stage centrifugation is carried out to improve the efficiency of separation. In two stage clarification, separation of okara is carried out in first stage while fine particles are separated in second stage. Efficient filtration enables the retention of fine particles in the aqueous phase which assists in achieving the suspension stability. Different studies have shown that filtration treatment through a decanter or continuous filtration system (20–80 μm) during the manufacturing process of non-dairy milks improves the physical stability of milk because of removal of suspended particles [68, 77]. These days membrane separation is becoming popular as it allows for efficient separation of aqueous portion from okara. In case of manufacturing milk from fat rich raw material, the surplus fat is separated using a separator as is done in dairy processing with cream separator.

3.6 Addition of ingredients

Once aqueous phase or base material is obtained upon extraction and filtration, other ingredients are blended in the aqueous phase in optimum levels for successful manufacturing of non-dairy milk alternatives. These ingredients include fat, vitamins, sugar, flavorings, salt, oils and stabilizers etc. Since physical poses a challenge for the successful development of any non-dairy milk alternative, different range of additives (emulsifiers and stabilizers) have been explored for their use in the milks. Various emulsifying agents such as alginates, gelatin, xanthan gum, gum Arabic, locust bean gum, and gellan gum in a range of 0.5 to 1% by weight demonstrate improved emulsion stability. The destabilization due to settling of solid particles in the emulsion may be overcome by addition of alkalizing agents, such as disodium phosphate or sodium bicarbonate. Maghsoudlou et al. [16] achieved stability of almond milk by using lecithin, modified starch and agar at 0.09%, 1.31% and 0.15% levels respectively. Nor (2012) suggested that addition of lecithin (0.03% w/w) at the time of the milling during manufacture of almond milk was beneficial for its stability. Hinds et al. [78] reported good results with the use of 0.02–0.04% carrageenan as stabilizer in peanut milk. Bernat et al. [20] established that addition of 0.05 g/100 mL xanthan gum before the heat processing was suitable for developing hazelnut milk substitute as it causes thickening of the hazelnut milk substitute and enhances the colloidal stability of the final product. Processing operations should be performed carefully, since non-dairy milk alternatives are fortified with minerals and vitamins which may compromise the stability of emulsion. This is because vitamins are known to exhibit instability in relation to environmental conditions like high temperature, light and exposure to oxygen. In addition, mineral fortification might result in destabilization of emulsion; therefore, their fortification is accompanied with the addition of chelators like citric and EDTA. Based on the dispersibility and solubility of mineral sources, the salts that are commonly used for the mineral fortification include ferric gluconate, ferric ammonium citrate and ferric pyrophosphate as iron sources and calcium citrate, tricalcium phosphate and calcium carbonate as calcium sources [79, 80].

3.7 Homogenization

Homogenization is employed for size reduction of the dispersed phase components in the range of 0.5–30 μm by application of shear forces. The particles of the dispersed phase like protein, starch, fiber, and other cellular materials tend to sediment at the bottom when allowed to stand for some time; however, with the contribution of size reduction due to homogenization and addition of emulsifying agents or hydrocolloids, the stabilization of suspension is achieved during manufacturing of non-dairy milk alternatives. For carrying out homogenization, a pressure range of 20–60 MPa has been employed to improve the suspension stability during manufacture of non-dairy milk alternatives like rice, hemp, coconut milk [81–83]. The process assists in subdivision of fat globules to prevent phase separation and facilitates development of creamier and homogenized product.

3.8 Heat treatment

High temperature treatments like pasteurization, sterilization or UHT are employed to increase the shelf life of non-dairy milks by destruction of microorganisms. Several studies have reported application of sterilization treatments at 121 °C for 15–30 min in various non- dairy milks like almond, soy and peanut milks [20, 81, 84, 85]. Also, UHT treatment in range of 134–140 °C for 2 to 20 seconds has been applied in different non-dairy milks like peanut, coconut and almond milk [69, 86]. However, high temperature treatments have been reported to destabilize non-dairy milk alternative by resulting in coagulation of proteins. This is because proteins at high temperatures unfold to expose nonpolar amino acid residues, which participate in protein–protein interactions and consequently, exhibit aggregation, sedimentation, or gelling phenomena. Homogenization treatment after heat processing improves suspension stability by disruption of aggregates and reduction of particle size distribution [87]. The gelling and thickening of non-dairy milks due to presence of starch is addressed by enzymatic treatment for hydrolyzing the carbohydrate. Apart from enhancing physical stability, these heat treatments cause simultaneous destruction of pathogenic microbes in plant based milk alternatives resulting in increased storage stability of these beverages. Maria *et al.* [88] reported that the pasteurization treatment improved the quality characteristics of almond milk. Likewise, Khodke *et al.* [89] evaluated the effect of sterilization on shelf life of soymilk. It was observed that sterilized samples were acceptable up to 90 days at ambient storage while at refrigerated storage, the shelf life of milk samples increased up to 170 days. In another study, the effect of ultra-high temperature treatment on quality attributes of soymilk was investigated. It was concluded that single step UHT process (143 °C/60 s) can result into a commercially sterile soymilk with thiamin retention up to 93%, reduced trypsin inhibitor activity and improved acceptable sensory properties [90].

3.9 Aseptic packaging

Aseptic packaging of non-dairy milk alternative into sterile packaging material is done to increase the shelf life of the product.

4. Influence of ingredients on the stability of non-dairy milk alternatives

4.1 Important ingredients

4.1.1 Fat phase

In formulation of nondairy milks, fats are standardized in products either as oil bodies obtained from plants or are fabricated synthetically through homogenization. Oil bodies consist of a fatty acid core made up of triacylglycerol and a surrounding monolayer of phospholipids and unique proteins (oleosins), thus which imparts a structure composition similar to that of milk fat globule [91]. Extraction of oil bodies from plant seeds is generally achieved by employing physical processes, like soaking and crushing to enable their separation from adjacent tissues [9]. Oleosins play important role in stabilization of oil bodies by preventing their coalescence [92], preventing their hydrolysis by phospholipases [20] and by balancing of PUFA to MUFA ratio [93]. Even though plant based milks are similar to bovine milk, they may exhibit a distinct flavor, perceptible as nutty or beany, and may not be as desirable compared to flavor of milk [24] which is mild and unique owing to its typical aroma and taste profile [94].

Owing to differences between the dispersed and continuous phases in colloidal dispersions, there is a net movement of particles between two phases under the influence of gravitational force; creaming occurs if density of particles in dispersed phase is lower compared to dispersion medium whereas sedimentation is evident, if the case is otherwise. Both these phenomena tend to destabilize a colloidal dispersion. With respect to non-dairy milks, oil bodies tend to exhibit upward movement, while raw material fractions and being heavier, tend to settle down at bottom resulting in sedimentation, and is usually overcome by homogenization. Besides, simulated fat may also be stabilized by use of emulsifiers and homogenization, thereby imparting to non-dairy milk alternatives the characteristics similar to those of bovine milk in terms of consistency, appearance, flavor, and mouthfeel [95]. Fat phase in plant based milks is derived from different oil sources like coconut, palm, sesame, flaxseed, sunflower, olive, and soybean which contribute to different attributes like solid fat index, melting/crystallization pattern, viscosity, sensory and physicochemical properties. These features have important implications on processing of non-dairy milk alternatives such as presence of molten state of fat prior to homogenization and subsequently size of oil droplets created. However, presence of unsaturated fatty acids in lipid phase of these milks renders them more prone to lipid oxidation and rancidity. In case the ratio of unsaturated to saturated fatty acids is high, it contributes positively to human health. Numerous studies over the years have associated the consumption of plant-based oils with beneficial health effects, such as anticarcinogenic, anti-inflammatory, anti-dyslipidemia, antioxidant and in particular, improved cardiac health status has been attributed to intake of unsaturated fatty acids [96, 97].

Because of the density difference that exists between the dispersed phase and continuous phase, gravitational separation is a phenomenon commonly observed in non-dairy milk alternatives. In order to overcome phase separation, the density difference may be diminished either by incorporating in the milk alternatives the fat with the higher solid fat index or by adding some weighting agents, surfactants, and biopolymers that can hold onto the oil bodies by completely surrounding them. Creaming is controlled either by formation of tenacious films by proteins on oil droplets or by increase of viscosity of the medium, for instance by addition of thickening agents like hydrocolloids and polysaccharides to the dispersion medium. It is because when there is incomplete coverage of the oil body, partial coalescence may take place, and aggregation occurs in the fat bodies in such cases. In general, the difference between the density of the aqueous and fat phase may be adjusted by the use of weighting agent like brominated vegetable oil. However, brominated oil is not commonly used in food emulsions since it has been shown to negatively affect the fat metabolism in rats [98]. Addition of brominated vegetable oil to regular vegetable oil at 25 wt% level diminishes the density difference between oil phase and aqueous phase [99]. Therefore, in order to achieve stability in milk alternatives, it is essential that lipid bodies may be designed either using fats with proper solid proportion to increase the density of dispersed phase or using suitable biopolymers for ensuring efficient coverage.

Flocculation is a phenomenon that involves the weak association of oil droplets due to net attractive forces resulting in formation of flocks. The characteristics of the flocks vary with the extent of the net force of attraction between the droplets and the oil volume fraction. In the cases when the net attractive forces are not strong, weak flocculation occurs, while large aggregates formation takes place due to strong attractive forces in the non-dairy milk alternatives. Flocculation of oil droplets leading to instability of the milk substitutes is governed by non-covalent interactions which may be either attractive (van der Waals forces) or repulsive (electrostatic forces and steric forces) and can be manipulated by using appropriate surfactant or biopolymer. The additive should present the properties capable of generating stronger repulsive forces compared to attractive forces to overcome aggregation. Surfactants, cationic or anionic in nature, upon formation of films, generate electrostatic forces, which stabilize the oil droplets against aggregation due to net repulsive forces. However, proteins are quite effective in stabilization against aggregation owing to strong steric repulsive forces associated with them.

Adsorption of fat droplets by proteins, causes overlap of the outer portion, which entails an osmotic pressure gradient; thereby, generating the repulsive forces which prevent droplet aggregation. This leads to decrease in entropy and overall stabilization of non-dairy milk.

4.1.2 Emulsion stabilizer

Since non-dairy milk alternatives are typically oil in water emulsions present in complex multi-component systems entailing fats, proteins and polysaccharides, additives, water, sugars, flavors, other small molecular-weight compounds, and are inherently unstable exhibiting phenomena like aggregation, creaming, coalescence, sedimentation. Therefore, it is essential to select relevant emulsion stabilizer (surfactants, emulsifiers and hydrocolloids) for improvising the stability of milk substitutes.

4.1.3 Different types of emulsifiers

Emulsifiers are usually surface active molecules that act by adsorbing to the surfaces of the droplets of dispersed phase by creating a protective coating around them to prevent their aggregation. They may be categorized in different forms like, low molecular weight compounds: synthetic (monoglycerides, polyglycerol esters) or natural (phospholipids) and high molecular weight biopolymers (proteins and polysaccharides) [100–102]. As to the stability of emulsions imparted by emulsifiers, it is mainly related to formation of viscoelastic films around dispersed droplets. Several studies have suggested that the main cause of stabilization of emulsions is related to the capacity of emulsifiers to efficiently adsorb on dispersed droplets, size of the droplets, concentration of emulsifier, and generation of repulsive forces as well as considerable reduction of surface tension [95, 103, 104].

4.1.4 Low molecular weight surfactants

Food industry has always shown interest in use of suitable emulsifiers in different formulations as various features of food are influenced like stability, mouthfeel, color, flavor, appearance, texture and shelf life of food. Low molecular weight surfactants (phospholipids, monoacylglycerol) are more efficient than proteins in reducing the interfacial tension between two phases of an emulsion because of their property of quick diffusion and adsorption to interface [105–114]. Proteins on account of being bulky are slow to diffuse to interface and hence, exhibit lower surface activity [105]. This might be attributed to the complex structure of a protein consisting of both hydrophobic and hydrophilic groups present variably throughout its primary structure, and as separate patches in tertiary structures with no clearly defined head and tail region, which, are essentially distinct in case of small surfactants. Moreover, due to the absence of conformational constraints for rearrangement at the interface, low molecular weight surfactants, at sufficiently high concentrations, are more successful than proteins prevent adsorption to oil droplets. In the case of emulsions, when the protein to surfactant ratio is low, protein displacement into the continuous phase takes place due to the surfactant molecule, based on the orogenic mechanism [102]. The mechanism suggests that the protein molecules are unable to pack completely, and adsorb homogeneously on the interface because of steric hindrance, thereby creating a void space. The void spaces are primarily occupied by the surfactant domains, which enlarge gradually creating pressures, that compress the nearby protein film, and finally resulting in its desorption in the continuous phase [113].

4.1.5 Proteins

Proteins adsorb to oil droplets by undergoing partial denaturation to position themselves such that buried hydrophobic residues are exposed to the oil phase while hydrophilic residues align towards the aqueous phase [13]. On diffusing to the interface, proteins form tenacious viscoelastic films which are not apparent with the surfactants. The films are able to withstand mechanical stress and impart electrostatic as well as steric stabilization corresponding to type of protein and solvent conditions [115]. In these emulsions, stability may also be attributed to presence of "loops and trains" in protein chain conformation [116–118].

Among the natural class of emulsifiers, proteins represent very interesting emulsifiers due to their film forming ability and amphipathic nature [119]. Generally, animal proteins have been popular in food industry due to their excellent emulsifying abilities. These include bovine milk and egg proteins such as casein, whey protein isolate, bovine serum albumin, ovalbumin, ovotransferrin [120–128]. However, during recent years, plant proteins have experienced increasing popularity among manufacturers because of their association with several beneficial properties such as stability, sustainability non-allergenicity, non-toxicity, low-cost, biodegradability, functional properties, and consumer acceptance due to the clean label status ascribed to them [129, 130]. Different plant proteins that have gained acceptance as emulsifier in various emulsion based food systems include soy proteins, chickpea, lentil, cowpea, pea proteins wheat gluten, rice glutelin and flaxseed protein [131–134]. In order to stabilize emulsions successfully, it is necessary that emulsifiers should not only prevent droplet aggregation but also be stable to exterior stresses like temperature, pH, salt concentrations, sugars, etc. Biopolymers such as proteins and polysaccharides vary in stability with respect to external conditions. Plant proteins (pea, legume, faba bean) lack stability at pH close to their pI, high temperature and high salt concentrations [135], whereas polysaccharides exhibit stability under similar conditions [136, 137].

Plant proteins are generally globular, like soy, pea, chickpea and cereal protein which undergo entropy changes on adsorption at interface through structural rearrangement in secondary and tertiary changes [138]. Likewise, in bovine milk, the whey proteins are globular in nature. β-lactoglobulin usually has much the unordered structure and α-lactalbumin helical structure. In contrast, the complex globular proteins from plant sources have ordered structure. For instance, the legume proteins such as glycinin and legumin have well-ordered and greatly conserved structure due to their rigid quaternary conformation. The quaternary structure undergoes conformational deformation at tertiary and secondary configuration on getting adsorbed at the interface. Proteins that have inherently disordered structures show better surface activity compared with ordered proteins. Unstructured proteins like casein, which have open random coil structure, exhibits conformational rearrangement as an emulsifier causing fast changes compared to globular proteins. Studies have shown that the competitive adsorption of proteins takes place at the oil–water interface in non-dairy milks, and among the mixture of proteins, some proteins adsorb more effectively compared to others based on their structure and the partitioning of hydrophobic and hydrophilic residues. Moreover, as plant proteins are globular, the exposed hydrophobic groups tend to adsorb to nonpolar groups of oil droplets in non-dairy alternatives, ensuing strong and long-range hydrophobic attractive forces, which overcome the repulsive forces, so that the net effect is particle aggregation. Therefore, the important aspect for control, in the viewpoint of the manufacturers to ensure the stability, is hydrophobicity, which is the inherent characteristic of the globular proteins, and besides, it becomes more pronounced due to thermal or surface denaturation. In order to prevent hydrophobic flocculation, it is necessary to select suitable proteins, which are less hydrophobic, and to avoid the processing procedures that encourage protein denaturation.

Therefore, to achieve stability in plant based milks, certain protein modification strategies may be applied. As discussed above, globular proteins are susceptible to denaturation, their surface activity and solubility may be altered during processing of non-dairy alternatives [139]. Physical, chemical and enzymatic modifications can be used to enhance the functional properties of proteins. In physical modification, proteins are subjected to controlled heating and shear conditions that lead to unfolding or partial denaturation of these macromolecules [140, 141]. Chemical modification involves acylation, sulfitolysis, phosphorylation and alkylation, which alters the secondary, tertiary and quaternary structure of proteins alongwith their hydrophilicity-hydrophobicity balance [142–144]. Enzymatic modification is an effective approach to enhance the functionality of proteins by means of hydrolysis and polymerization reactions catalyzed by proteases (pepsin, chymotrypsin & trypsin) and transglutaminases. The controlled hydrolysis generates smaller oil droplets than intact proteins and also increases the emulsifying activity index [145, 146].

4.1.6 Hydrocolloids

For achieving stability in the non-dairy milk alternatives, the addition of hydrocolloids like guar gum, locust bean gum, Gum Arabic, carrageenan, xanthan gum, and so on, is often carried out to prevent creaming and phase separation [147–149]. The charge on polysaccharides impacts their ability to inhibit the aggregation of oil bodies or fat droplets as well as of proteins by the formation of a protective coating around them. For instance, carrageenan, an anionic hydrocolloid, adsorbs to cationic regions on surfaces of aggregating proteins and hence, prevents aggregation near their isoelectric point by creating strong electrostatic or steric repulsive forces [150]. However, studies suggest that while hydrocolloids are capable of promoting stability at high concentrations, they tend to create instability in emulsions at low concentrations. Different mechanisms have been hypothesized to elucidate this phenomenon. When two droplets covered with a surfactant are in close vicinity, a link between the droplets develops which creates a connection between droplets [151, 152]. Development of numerous contacts of this type tend to encourage flocculation and increase the creaming rate. This is generally identified as "bridging flocculation," and it is more common when the hydrocolloid is a weak emulsifier [153]. Therefore, the success of emulsion stabilization depends on the choice of proper biopolymers that lack the attraction to the dispersed phase droplets.

Other mechanism, proposed as "depletion flocculation," was initially suggested by Asakura and Oosawa [154, 155] and was supported by many scientists later on [156–158]. According to mechanism, upon addition of any nonadsorbing hydrocolloid to a reasonably concentrated emulsion, elimination of the hydrocolloid might occur in the area between droplets, because of its hydrodynamic size, and thereby leads to development of local osmotic pressure gradient. The osmotic force results in the aggregation of oil droplets. The extent of the attractive force is related to the molecular weight and conformation of the hydrocolloid and varies proportionally with the concentration of the nonadsorbing hydrocolloid. Such kind of instability may be prevented by mixing the polysaccharide in less quantity so that aggregation does not occur.

4.2 Advanced processing techniques in relation to stability of non-dairy milk alternatives

4.2.1 Ultra high pressure homogenization (UHPH)

Ultra high pressure homogenization is an emerging technology which can be utilized to enhance the stability of plant based milk alternatives by reducing the colloidal particles. UHPH produces more uniform sized particles and improves the physicochemical characteristics of food products without affecting their nutritional properties [159]. Apart from reducing the particle size, this technique can also be applied to improve the shelf life of plant based milk alternatives by means of simultaneous destruction of microorganism [160]. UHPH involves the use of high pressure in the range of 200–600 MPa and temperatures between 30 and 85 °C [161]. The use of UHPH also displays an important role in reduction of allergenic character of plant-based milk alternatives. Briviba *et al.* [21] investigated the effect of UHPH treatment (350 MPa at 80 °C) on physicochemical properties of almond milk. No significant reduction in vitamin B_1 and B_2 contents was reported while the mean particle size increased threefold. A reduction (99.8%) in almond protein antigens response was also observed. The effect of UHPH treatment (300 MPa at 80 °C) and UHT treatment (142 °C, 6 s) on microbiological, physical and sensorial properties of soymilk was evaluated [162]. The study showed a reduction in hydroperoxide index and microbial growth throughout the storage period for both treatments. Slight differences in sensory characteristics were observed between treatments; however, panelists did not consider these differences to compare treatments.

4.2.2 Pulsed electric field (PFF)

Pulsed electric field is another promising technology that involves the use of short electricity pulses to inactivate microorganisms in food products while causing minimal changes in color, flavor, taste and nutritional components [163]. In this technology, food is placed between two electrodes and electric fields (5–50 KV/Cm) are generated with the help of short high voltage pulses (microseconds) between the electrodes. The voltage range can be used for development of non-dairy milk alternatives according to the requirements of size reduction. The experiment carried out by Xiang [164] investigated the effect of pulsed electric field treatments with different electric field intensities and number of pulses on structural modification and rheological properties of soymilk. Pulse electric field treatments at electric field intensities (18, 20 and 22 kV/cm) and number of pulses (25, 59, 75 and 100) increased the apparent viscosity of soymilk (6.62 to 7.46) as compared to control (not treated). The changes were attributed to the PEF induced coagulation of the soy protein and reduction in size of fat globules and their distribution in soy milk. Similarly, Cortes *et al.* [165] explored the impact of treatment time (100–475 μs) and electric field intensity (20–35 kV/cm) on the quality attributes of horchata (a Spanish vegetable beverage) during 5 days at refrigerated storage (2–4 °C). The study revealed that PEF treatment significantly decreased the peroxidase activity and a negative correlation was found among peroxidase activity and pH. The increase in pH was proportional to increasing treatment time in the same electric field intensity.

4.2.3 Ultrasound processing

Ultrasound processing is an effective non-thermal technology applied for processing and preservation of foods. Ultrasound processing is based on the phenomenon of acoustic cavitation i.e. rapid expansion and contraction of bubbles of gas/vapors. This generates intense local heating and high pressures that causes disintegration of microbial cells and reduces the size of colloidal particles as well. In the study conducted by Iswarin and Permadi [166], the effect of ultrasound on droplet diameter of coconut milk was evaluated. The beverage was subjected to different combinations of power levels (2.5 to 7.0 W) and exposure times (5 to 25 minutes) and a reduction in particle size of coconut-based milk was observed as the US power and time increased. Similarly, Maghsoudlou et al. [19] studied the effect of ultrasonication treatment on physical stability of almond milk when applied at a power level of 300 W for the time periods of 0, 2.5 and 5 min. It was revealed that exposure time for 5 minutes was sufficient to manufacture a desirable product. The study demonstrated a decrease in sedimentation tendency of milk as well as decreased viscosity of almond milk. The improved stability has been attributed to cavitation induced fragmentation of colloidal polysaccharide molecules into smaller size particles. Size reduction of plant cellular material keeps them in suspension and hence, aids in improved stability.

5. Future prospect and conclusion

Being a fast-growing segment of food market, the plant-based milk substitutes need to be extensively explored by using advanced processing and innovative technologies to produce a nutritionally complete beverage with high overall acceptability. Plant-based milk substitutes lack cholesterol, milk allergens, lactose, antibiotics, and saturated fatty acids that make them convenient to be considered nutritious, economical, health promoting, palatable dairy-free beverage. To meet consumer's needs, it is essential to produce high quality beverages having good physical stability and desirable sensory attributes. Addition of stabilizers and processing are crucial steps in determining the stability and shelf life of plant-based milk alternatives. Manufacturers and consumers are more interested in clean label options for use as additives. Since synthetic stabilizers are generally added for improving the stability of milk substitutes, the natural substitutes could present a plausible solution to consumers. Some advanced food processing techniques including ultra-high pressure homogenization, pulsed electric field processing, ultrasound processing and high pressure processing can be employed to overcome instability factors responsible for limiting success of these beverages. Progressive efforts are required for improving product quality through research and development activities.

Author details

Jyotika Dhankhar* and Preeti Kundu
Department of Food Technology, Maharishi Dayanand University, Rohtak, Haryana, India

*Address all correspondence to: jyotika.ft@mdurohtak.ac.in

References

[1] Poore J, Nemecek T. Reducing food's environmental impacts through producers and consumers. Science. 2018 Jun 1;360(6392):987-992.

[2] Willett W, Rockström J, Loken B, Springmann M, Lang T, Vermeulen S, Garnett T, Tilman D, DeClerck F, Wood A, Jonell M. Food in the Anthropocene: the EAT–Lancet Commission on healthy diets from sustainable food systems. The Lancet. 2019 Feb 2;393(10170):447-492.

[3] SwagertyJr DL, Walling A, Klein RM. Lactose intolerance. American family physician. 2002 May 1;65(9):1845.

[4] Bode S, Gudmand-Høyer E. Incidence and clinical significance of lactose malabsorption in adult coeliac disease. Scandinavian journal of gastroenterology. 1988 Jan 1;23(4):484-488.

[5] Kneepkens CF, Meijer Y. Clinical practice. Diagnosis and treatment of cow's milk allergy. European journal of pediatrics. 2009 Aug 1;168(8):891-896.

[6] Omoni AO, Aluko RE. Soybean foods and their benefits: potential mechanisms of action. Nutrition reviews. 2005 Aug 1;63(8):272-283.

[7] Wien M, Oda K, Sabaté J. A randomized controlled trial to evaluate the effect of incorporating peanuts into an American Diabetes Association meal plan on the nutrient profile of the total diet and cardiometabolic parameters of adults with type 2 diabetes. Nutrition journal. 2014 Dec 1;13(1):10.

[8] Biswas S, Sircar D, Mitra A, De B. Phenolic constituents and antioxidant properties of some varieties of Indian rice. Nutrition & Food Science. 2011 Mar 29.41(2):123-135.

[9] Nikiforidis CV, Matsakidou A, Kiosseoglou V. Composition, properties and potential food applications of natural emulsions and cream materials based on oil bodies. RSC Advances. 2014;4(48):25067-25078.

[10] Park YW, editor. Bioactive components in milk and dairy products. John Wiley & Sons; 2009 Sep 15.

[11] Chalupa-Krebzdak S, Long CJ, Bohrer BM. Nutrient density and nutritional value of milk and plant-based milk alternatives. International dairy journal. 2018 Dec 1;87:84-92.

[12] Deeth H. Optimum thermal processing for extended shelf-life (ESL) milk. Foods. 2017 Nov;6(11):102.

[13] Walstra P, Walstra P, Wouters JT, Geurts TJ. Dairy science and technology. CRC press; 2005 Sep 29.

[14] Codina-Torrella I, Guamis B, Zamora A, Quevedo JM, Trujillo AJ. Microbiological stabilization of tiger nuts' milk beverage using ultra-high pressure homogenization. A preliminary study on microbial shelf-life extension. Food microbiology. 2018 Feb 1;69:143-150.

[15] Dhakal S, Liu C, Zhang Y, Roux KH, Sathe SK, Balasubramaniam VM. Effect of high pressure processing on the immunoreactivity of almond milk. Food Research International. 2014 Aug 1;62:215-222.

[16] Gul O, Saricaoglu FT, Mortas M, Atalar I, Yazici F. Effect of high pressure homogenization (HPH) on microstructure and rheological properties of hazelnut milk. Innovative Food Science & Emerging Technologies. 2017 Jun 1;41:411-420.

[17] Iorio MC, Bevilacqua A, Corbo MR, Campaniello D, Sinigaglia M, Altieri C. A case study on the use of ultrasound for the inhibition of

Escherichia coli O157: H7 and Listeria monocytogenes in almond milk. Ultrasonicssonochemistry. 2019 Apr 1; 52:477-483.

[18] Lu X, Chen J, Zheng M, Guo J, Qi J, Chen Y, Miao S, Zheng B. Effect of high-intensity ultrasound irradiation on the stability and structural features of coconut-grain milk composite systems utilizing maize kernels and starch with different amylose contents. Ultrasonicssonochemistry. 2019 Jul 1; 55:135-148.

[19] Maghsoudlou Y, Alami M, Mashkour M, Shahraki MH. Optimization of ultrasound-assisted stabilization and formulation of almond milk. Journal of Food Processing and Preservation. 2016 Oct;40(5):828-839.

[20] Bernat N, Chafer M, Rodríguez-García J, Chiralt A, González-Martínez C. Effect of high pressure homogenisation and heat treatment on physical properties and stability of almond and hazelnut milks. LWT-Food Science and Technology. 2015 Jun 1; 62(1):488-496.

[21] Briviba K, Gräf V, Walz E, Guamis B, Butz P. Ultra high pressure homogenization of almond milk: Physico-chemical and physiological effects. Food Chemistry. 2016 Feb 1;192:82-89.

[22] Maestri DM, Labuckas DO, Guzmán CA. Chemical and physical characteristics of a soybean beverage with improved flavor by addition of ethylenediaminetetraacetic acid. Grasas y aceites. 2000 Oct 30;51(5):316-319.

[23] Civille GV, SZCZESNIAK AS. Guidelines to training a texture profile panel. Journal of texture studies. 1973 Jun;4(2):204-223.

[24] Sethi S, Tyagi SK, Anurag RK. Plant-based milk alternatives an emerging segment of functional beverages: a review. Journal of food science and technology. 2016 Sep 1; 53(9):3408-3423.

[25] Do DT, Singh J, Oey I, Singh H. Biomimetic plant foods: Structural design and functionality. Trends in Food Science & Technology. 2018 Dec 1;82:46-59.

[26] Debruyne I. Soy base extract: soymilk and dairy alternatives. In: Riaz MN, editors. Soy applications in foods. Boca Raton, Florida, U.S.A: Taylor & Francis; 2006. p. 111-134.

[27] Perren R, Escher FE. Impact of roasting on nut quality In: Harris LJ, editors. Improving the Safety and Quality of Nuts. Cambridge: Woodhead Publishing.; 2013. p. 173-197.

[28] Baik BK, Han IH. Cooking, roasting, and fermentation of chickpeas, lentils, peas, and soybeans for fortification of leavened bread. Cereal Chemistry. 2012 Nov;89(6):269-275.

[29] Rehman ZU, Shah WH. Thermal heat processing effects on antinutrients, protein and starch digestibility of food legumes. Food chemistry. 2005 Jun 1;91(2):327-331.

[30] Aguilera Y, Esteban RM, Benitez V, Molla E, Martin-Cabrejas MA. Starch, functional properties, and microstructural characteristics in chickpea and lentil as affected by thermal processing. Journal of agricultural and food chemistry. 2009 Nov 25;57(22):10682-10688.

[31] Chung HJ, Liu Q, Donner E, Hoover R, Warkentin TD, Vandenberg B. Composition, molecular structure, properties, and in vitro digestibility of starches from newly released Canadian pulse cultivars. Cereal Chemistry. 2008 Jul;85(4):471-479.

[32] O'Brien S, Wang YJ. Susceptibility of annealed starches to hydrolysis by α-amylase and glucoamylase.

Carbohydrate polymers. 2008 Jun 10;72(4):597-607.

[33] Navicha WB, Hua Y, Masamba K, Kong X, Zhang C. Optimization of soybean roasting parameters in developing nutritious and lipoxygenase free soymilk. Journal of Food Measurement and Characterization. 2017 Dec;11(4):1899-1908.

[34] GALVEZ FC, RESURRECCION AV, KOEHLER PE. Optimization of Processing of Peanut Beverage 1. Journal of Sensory Studies. 1990 Jun;5(1):1-7.

[35] Akubor PI, Ogbadu RL. Effects of processing methods on the quality and acceptability of melon milk. Plant Foods for Human Nutrition. 2003 Mar;58(1):1-6.

[36] Zaaboul F, Raza H, Cao C, Yuanfa L. The impact of roasting, high pressure homogenization and sterilization on peanut milk and its oil bodies. Food chemistry. 2019 May 15;280:270-277.

[37] Ahmadian-Kouchaksaraei Z, Varidi M, Varidi MJ, Pourazarang H. Influence of processing conditions on the physicochemical and sensory properties of sesame milk: A novel nutritional beverage. LWT-Food science and Technology. 2014 Jun 1;57(1):299-305.

[38] Murugkar DA, Jha K. Effect of sprouting on nutritional and functional characteristics of soybean. J Food Sci Technol. 2009 May 1;46(3):240-243.

[39] Achouri A, Boye JI, Zamani Y. Soybean variety and storage effects on soymilk flavour and quality. International Journal of Food Science & Technology. 2008 Jan;43(1):82-90.

[40] Giri SK, Mangaraj S. Processing influences on composition and quality attributes of soymilk and its powder. Food Engineering Reviews. 2012 Sep 1;4(3):149-164.

[41] Lv YC, Song HL, Li X, Wu L, Guo ST. Influence of blanching and grinding process with hot water on beany and non-beany flavor in soymilk. Journal of Food Science. 2011 Jan;76(1):S20–S25.

[42] MacLeod G, Ames J, Betz NL. Soy flavor and its improvement. Critical Reviews in Food Science & Nutrition. 1988 Jan 1;27(4):219-400.

[43] Gardner HW. How the lipoxygenase pathway affects the organoleptic properties of fresh fruit and vegetables. In: Min DB, Smouse TH, editors. Flavor chemistry of lipid foods. American Oil Chemists' Society. 1989. p 98-15.

[44] Kundu P, Dhankhar J, Sharma A. Development of non dairy milk alternative using soymilk and almond milk. Current Research in Nutrition and Food Science Journal. 2018 Apr 20;6(1):203-210.

[45] Lee C, Beuchat LR. Chemical, physical and sensory characteristics of peanut milk as affected by processing conditions. Journal of Food Science. 1992 Mar;57(2):401-405.

[46] Wareing PW, Nicolaides L, Twiddy DR. Nuts and nut products. In: Lund BM, Baird-Parker TC, Gould GW, editors. The Microbiological Safety and Quality of Food. Gaithersburg, USA: Aspen Publishers; 2000. p. 919-940.

[47] Jain P, Yadav DN, Rajput H, Bhatt DK. Effect of pressure blanching on sensory and proximate composition of peanut milk. Journal of food science and technology. 2013 Jun;50(3):605-608.

[48] Joshi M, Adhikari B, Panozzo J, Aldred P. Water uptake and its impact on the texture of lentils (Lens culinaris). Journal of Food Engineering. 2010 Sep 1;100(1):61-69.

[49] Decker EA, Rose DJ, Stewart D. Processing of oats and the impact of processing operations on nutrition and health benefits. British Journal of Nutrition. 2014 Oct;112(S2):S58–S64.

[50] Khandelwal S, Udipi SA, Ghugre P. Polyphenols and tannins in Indian pulses: Effect of soaking, germination and pressure cooking. Food Research International. 2010 Mar 1;43(2):526-530.

[51] Pan Z, Tangratanavalee W. Characteristics of soybeans as affected by soaking conditions. LWT-Food Science and Technology. 2003 Feb 1;36(1):143-151.

[52] Kluczkovski A, Lima N, Oliveira MK. Brazil nut powdered milk properties. Journal of Food Processing and Preservation. 2017 Oct;41(5):e13147.

[53] Chen Y, Lu Y, Yu A, Kong X, Hua Y. Stable mixed beverage is produced from walnut milk and raw soymilk by homogenization with subsequent heating. Food Science and Technology Research. 2014;20(3):583-591.

[54] Kizzie-Hayford N, Jaros D, Schneider Y, Rohm H. Characteristics of tiger nut milk: effects of milling. International Journal of Food Science & Technology. 2015 Feb;50(2):381-388.

[55] Cho SH, Lee BH, Eun JB. Physicochemical properties of dry- and semi-wet-milled rice flours after fermentation by Lactobacillus amylovorus. Journal of Cereal Science. 2019 Jan 1;85:15-19.

[56] Maindarkar S, Dubbelboer A, Meuldijk J, Hoogland H, Henson M. Prediction of emulsion drop size distributions in colloid mills. Chemical Engineering Science. 2014 Oct 18;118:114-125.

[57] Li X, Kokawa M, Kitamura Y. Influence of micro wet milling parameters on the processing of Komatsuna (Brassica rapa var. perviridis) juice with rich phosphatidic acid. Journal of food engineering. 2018 Jan 1;217:50-57.

[58] Lopes M, Pierrepont C, Duarte CM, Filipe A, Medronho B, Sousa I. Legume beverages from chickpea and lupin, as new milk alternatives. Foods. 2020 Oct;9(10):1458.

[59] Vishwanathan KH, Singh V, Subramanian R. Wet grinding characteristics of soybean for soymilk extraction. Journal of Food Engineering. 2011 Sep 1;106(1):28-34.

[60] Roy F, Boye JI, Simpson BK. Bioactive proteins and peptides in pulse crops: Pea, chickpea and lentil. Food research international. 2010 Mar 1;43(2):432-442.

[61] Papalamprou EM, Doxastakis GI, Kiosseoglou V. Chickpea protein isolates obtained by wet extraction as emulsifying agents. Journal of the Science of Food and Agriculture. 2010 Jan 30;90(2):304-313.

[62] Donsì F, Senatore B, Huang Q, Ferrari G. Development of novel pea protein-based nanoemulsions for delivery of nutraceuticals. Journal of Agricultural and Food Chemistry. 2010 Oct 13;58(19):10653-10660.

[63] Sousa A, Kopf KA. Nutritional Implications of an Increasing Consumption of Non-Dairy Plant-Based Beverages Instead of Cow's Milk in Switzerland. Advances in Dairy Research. 2017;5(04):1-7.

[64] de Moura JM, Campbell K, Mahfuz A, Jung S, Glatz CE, Johnson L. Enzyme-assisted aqueous extraction of oil and protein from soybeans and cream de-emulsification. Journal of the American Oil Chemists' Society. 2008 Oct;85(10):985-995.

[65] Abdullah AL, Sulaiman NM, Aroua MK, Noor MM. Response surface optimization of conditions for clarification of carambola fruit juice using a commercial enzyme. Journal of Food Engineering. 2007 Jul 1;81(1):65-71.

[66] Mutlu M, Sarioğlu K, Demir N, Ercan MT, Acar J. The use of commercial pectinase in fruit juice industry. Part I: viscosimetric determination of enzyme activity. Journal of Food Engineering. 1999 Aug 1;41(3-4):147-150.

[67] Jung S, Lamsal BP, Stepien V, Johnson LA, Murphy PA. Functionality of soy protein produced by enzyme-assisted extraction. Journal of the American Oil Chemists' Society. 2006 Jan;83(1):71-78.

[68] Rosenthal A, Deliza R, Cabral LM, Cabral LC, Farias CA, Domingues AM. Effect of enzymatic treatment and filtration on sensory characteristics and physical stability of soymilk. Food Control. 2003 Apr 1;14(3):187-192.

[69] Rustom IY, López-Leiva MH, Nair BM. Nutritional, sensory and physicochemical properties of peanut beverage sterilized under two different UHT conditions. Food Chemistry. 1996 May 1;56(1):45-53.

[70] Mitchell CR, Mitchell PR, Nissenbaum R, inventors; Mitchell Cheryl R, Mitchell Pat R, assignee. Nutritional rice milk product. United States patent US 4,894,242. 1990 Jan 16.

[71] Tano-Debrah, K., Asiamah, K., Sakyi-Dawson, E. and Budu, A.S., 2005. Effect of malt enzyme treatment on the nutritional and physicochemical characteristics of cowpea-peanut milk. In *Proceedings of the 1st International Edible Legume Conference in conjuction with the IVth World Cowpea Congress, Durban, South Africa, 17-21 April 2005* (pp. 1-7). University of Pretoria.

[72] Jeske S, Zannini E, Arendt EK. Past, present and future: The strength of plant-based dairy substitutes based on gluten-free raw materials. Food Research International. 2018 Aug 1;110:42-51.

[73] Apar DK, Özbek B. α-Amylase inactivation during rice starch hydrolysis. Process Biochemistry. 2005 Mar 1;40(3-4):1367-1379.

[74] Deswal A, Deora NS, Mishra HN. Optimization of enzymatic production process of oat milk using response surface methodology. Food and Bioprocess Technology. 2014 Feb;7(2):610-618.

[75] Diarra K, Nong ZG, Jie C. Peanut milk and peanut milk based products production: a review. Critical reviews in food science and nutrition. 2005 Jul 1;45(5):405-423.

[76] Lindahl L, Ahlden I, Oste R, Sjoholm I, inventors; Lindahl, Lennart, Ahlden, Inger, Oeste, Rickard, Sjoeholm, assignee. Homogeneous and stable cereal suspension and a method of making the same. United States patent US 5,686,123. 1997 Nov 11.

[77] Haumann BF. Soymilk: New processing, packaging. Expand markets. J. Am. Oil Chem. Soc. 1984;61:17884.

[78] Hinds MJ, Chinnan MS, Beuchat LR. Particle size distribution in a heat-processed beverage prepared from roasted peanuts. Food research international. 1997 Jan 1;30(1):59-64..

[79] Zhang H, Önning G, Öste R, Gramatkovski E, Hulthén L. Improved iron bioavailability in an oat-based beverage: the combined effect of citric acid addition, dephytinization and iron supplementation. European journal of nutrition. 2007 Mar;46(2):95-102.

[80] Zhang H, Önning G, Triantafyllou AÖ, Öste R. Nutritional

properties of oat-based beverages as affected by processing and storage. Journal of the Science of Food and Agriculture. 2007 Sep;87(12):2294-2301.

[81] Lee SW, Rhee C. Processing suitability of a rice and pine nut (Pinus koraiensis) beverage. Food hydrocolloids. 2003 May 1;17(3):379-385.

[82] Wang Q, Jiang J, Xiong YL. High pressure homogenization combined with pH shift treatment: A process to produce physically and oxidatively stable hemp milk. Food Research International. 2018 Apr 1;106:487-494.

[83] Tangsuphoom N, Coupland JN. Effect of heating and homogenization on the stability of coconut milk emulsions. Journal of food science. 2005 Oct;70(8):e466–e470.

[84] Quasem JM, Mazahreh AS, Abu-Alruz K. Development of vegetable based milk from decorticated sesame (Sesamum indicum). American Journal of Applied Sciences. 2009;6(5):888-896.

[85] Manzoor MF, Manzoor A, Siddique R, Ahmad N. Nutritional and Sensory Properties of Cashew Seed (Anacardium occidentale) Milk. Modern Concepts & Developments in Agronomy. 2017;1(1):1-4.

[86] Khuenpet K, Jittanit W, Hongha N, Pairojkul S. UHT skim coconut milk production and its quality. InSHS Web of Conferences 2016 (Vol. 23, p. 03002). EDP Sciences.

[87] Mäkinen OE, Uniacke-Lowe T, O'Mahony JA, Arendt EK. Physicochemical and acid gelation properties of commercial UHT-treated plant-based milk substitutes and lactose free bovine milk. Food Chemistry. 2015 Feb 1;168:630-638.

[88] Maria MF, Victoria AT. Influence of processing treatments on quality of vegetable milk from almond (Terminalia catappa) kernels. ACTA Sci. Nutr. Health. 2018;2(6):37-42.

[89] Khodke SU, Shinde KS, Yenge GB. A study on the storage of sterilized soymilk. International journal of farm sciences. 2014;4(4):166-179.

[90] Kwok KC, Liang HH, Niranjan K. Optimizing conditions for thermal processes of soy milk. Journal of agricultural and food chemistry. 2002 Aug 14;50(17):4834-4838.

[91] Michalski MC. Specific molecular and colloidal structures of milk fat affecting lipolysis, absorption and postprandial lipemia. European Journal of Lipid Science and Technology. 2009 May;111(5):413-431.

[92] Huang XL, Catignani GL, Swaisgood HE. Improved emulsifying properties of β-barrel domain peptides obtained by membrane-fractionation of a limited tryptic hydrolysate of β-lactoglobulin. Journal of Agricultural and Food Chemistry. 1996 Nov 14;44(11):3437-3443.

[93] Prieto AF. Consideraciones prácticas acerca de los sistemas de producción de caprino de leche en el sur de España. InProducción ovina y caprina: XVIII Jornadas de la Sociedad Española de Ovinotecnia y Caprinotecnia 1994 (pp. 45-58). Universidad de Castilla-La Mancha.

[94] Drake MA. Invited review: Sensory analysis of dairy foods. Journal of dairy science. 2007 Nov 1;90(11):4925-4937.

[95] McClements DJ, Gumus CE. Natural emulsifiers—Biosurfactants, phospholipids, biopolymers, and colloidal particles: Molecular and physicochemical basis of functional performance. Advances in Colloid and interface Science. 2016 Aug 1;234:3-26.

[96] Estruch R, Ros E, Salas-Salvado J, Covas MI, Corella D, Aros F, Gomez-Gracia E, Ruiz-Gutierrez V, Fiol M, Lapetra J, Lamuela-Raventos RM. Primary prevention of cardiovascular disease with a Mediterranean diet. New England Journal of Medicine. 2013 Apr 4;368(14):1279-1290.

[97] Kelly JH, Sabaté J. Nuts and coronary heart disease: an epidemiological perspective. British Journal of Nutrition. 2006 Nov;96(S2):S61–S67.

[98] Lombardo YB, Chicco A, Basílico MZ, Bernal C, Gutman R. Effect of brominated vegetable oils on heart lipid metabolism. Lipids. 1985 Jul 1;20(7):425-432.

[99] Chanamai R, McClements DJ. Impact of weighting agents and sucrose on gravitational separation of beverage emulsions. Journal of Agricultural and Food Chemistry. 2000 Nov 20;48(11):5561-5565.

[100] Goldstein A, Seetharaman K. Effect of a novel monoglyceride stabilized oil in water emulsion shortening on cookie properties. Food Research International. 2011 Jun 1;44(5):1476-1481.

[101] Tual A, Bourles E, Barey P, Houdoux A, Desprairies M, Courthaudon JL. Effect of surfactant sucrose ester on physical properties of dairy whipped emulsions in relation to those of O/W interfacial layers. Journal of colloid and interface science. 2006 Mar 15;295(2):495-503.

[102] Su J, Flanagan J, Hemar Y, Singh H. Synergistic effects of polyglycerol ester of polyricinoleic acid and sodium caseinate on the stabilisation of water–oil–water emulsions. Food Hydrocolloids. 2006 Mar 1;20(2-3):261-268.

[103] Bouyer E, Mekhloufi G, Rosilio V, Grossiord JL, Agnely F. Proteins, polysaccharides, and their complexes used as stabilizers for emulsions: alternatives to synthetic surfactants in the pharmaceutical field?. International journal of pharmaceutics. 2012 Oct 15;436(1-2):359-378.

[104] Gunning PA, Hennock MS, Howe AM, Mackie AR, Richmond P, Robins MM. Stability of oil-in-water emulsions. The effect of dispersed phase and polysaccharide on creaming. Colloids and surfaces. 1986 Sep 15;20(1-2):65-80.

[105] Kiosseoglou V, Perdikis A. Stability of bovine serum albumin-stabilized olive oil-in-water emulsions and the role of the oil minor surface-active lipids. Food hydrocolloids. 1994 Mar 1;8(1):27-32.

[106] Tomas A, Courthaudon JL, Paquet D, Lorient D. Effect of surfactant on some physico-chemical properties of dairy oil-in-water emulsions. Food Hydrocolloids. 1994 Dec 1;8(6):543-553.

[107] Dickinson E, Hong ST. Surface Coverage of. beta.-Lactoglobulin at the Oil-Water Interface: Influence of Protein Heat Treatment and Various Emulsifiers. Journal of Agricultural and Food Chemistry. 1994 Aug;42(8):1602-1606.

[108] Fang Y, Dalgleish DG. Competitive adsorption between dioleoylphosphatidylcholine and sodium caseinate on oil– water interfaces. Journal of Agricultural and Food Chemistry. 1996 Jan 18;44(1):59-64.

[109] Dalgleish DG, Srinivasan M, Singh H. Surface properties of oil-in-water emulsion droplets containing casein and Tween 60. Journal of Agricultural and Food Chemistry. 1995 Sep;43(9):2351-2355.

[110] Euston SE, Singh H, Munro PA, Dalgleish DG. Competitive adsorption between sodium caseinate and

oil-soluble and water-soluble surfactants in oil-in-water emulsions. Journal of food science. 1995 Sep;60(5):1124-1131.

[111] Euston SE, Singh H, Munro PA, Dalgleish DG. Oil-in-water emulsions stabilized by sodium caseinate or whey protein isolate as influenced by glycerol monostearate. Journal of food science. 1996 Sep;61(5):916-920.

[112] Gunning PA, Mackie AR, Gunning AP, Wilde PJ, Woodward NC, Morris VJ. The effect of surfactant type on protein displacement from the air–water interface. Food Hydrocolloids. 2004 May 1;18(3):509-515.

[113] Mackie AR, Gunning AP, Pugnaloni LA, Dickinson E, Wilde PJ, Morris VJ. Growth of surfactant domains in protein films. Langmuir. 2003 Jul 22;19(15):6032-6038.

[114] Mackie AR, Gunning AP, Wilde PJ, Morris VJ. Competitive displacement of β-lactoglobulin from the air/water interface by sodium dodecyl sulfate. Langmuir. 2000 Oct 17;16(21):8176-8181.

[115] Tcholakova S, Denkov ND, Ivanov IB, Campbell B. Coalescence stability of emulsions containing globular milk proteins. Advances in colloid and interface science. 2006 Nov 16;123:259-293.

[116] Dalgleish DG. Adsorption of protein and the stability of emulsions. Trends Food SciTechnol. 1997: 8:1-6.

[117] Wilde PJ. Interfaces: their role in foam and emulsion behaviour. Current Opinion in Colloid & Interface Science. 2000 Jul 1;5(3-4):176-181.

[118] Dickinson E. Milk protein interfacial layers and the relationship to emulsion stability and rheology. Colloids and Surfaces B: Biointerfaces. 2001 Mar 1;20(3):197-210.

[119] Foegeding EA, Davis JP. Food protein functionality: A comprehensive approach. Food Hydrocolloids. 2011 Dec 1;25(8):1853-1864.

[120] Hu, M., McClements, J., & Decker, E. A. (2003). Lipid oxidation in corn oil-in-water emulsions stabilized by casein, whey protein isolate, and soy protein isolate. Journal of Agricultural and Food Chemistry, 51, 1696-1700.

[121] Li JL, Cheng YQ, Wang P, Zhao WT, Yin LJ, Saito M. A novel improvement in whey protein isolate emulsion stability: Generation of an enzymatically cross-linked beet pectin layer using horseradish peroxidase. Food Hydrocolloids. 2012 Mar 1;26(2):448-455.

[122] Ye A, Singh H. Heat stability of oil-in-water emulsions formed with intact or hydrolysed whey proteins: influence of polysaccharides. Food hydrocolloids. 2006 Mar 1;20(2-3):269-276.

[123] Dalgleish DG. The sizes and conformations of the proteins in adsorbed layers of individual caseins on latices and in oil-in-water emulsions. Colloids and Surfaces B: Biointerfaces. 1993 May 14;1(1):1-8.

[124] Mulvihill DM, Murphy PC. Surface active and emulsifying properties of caseins/caseinates as influenced by state of aggregation. International Dairy Journal. 1991 Jan 1;1(1):13-37.

[125] Galazka VB, Dickinson E, Ledward DA. Emulsifying properties of ovalbumin in mixtures with sulphated polysaccharides: effects of pH, ionic strength, heat and high-pressure treatment. Journal of the Science of Food and Agriculture. 2000 Jun;80(8):1219-1229.

[126] Mine Y, Noutomi T, Haga N. Emulsifying and structural properties of ovalbumin. Journal of Agricultural and Food Chemistry. 1991:39:443-446.

[127] Nakamura S, Kato A, Kobayashi K. Enhanced antioxidative effect of ovalbumin due to covalent binding of polysaccharides. Journal of Agricultural and Food Chemistry. 1992 Nov;40(11):2033-2037.

[128] Castelain C, Genot C. Partition of adsorbed and nonadsorbed bovine serum albumin in dodecane-in-water emulsions calculated from front-face intrinsic fluorescence measurements. Journal of agricultural and food chemistry. 1996 Jul 18;44(7):1635-1640.

[129] Yin B, Deng W, Xu K, Huang L, Yao P. Stable nano-sized emulsions produced from soy protein and soy polysaccharide complexes. Journal of colloid and interface science. 2012 Aug 15;380(1):51-59.

[130] Doublier JL, Garnier C, Renard D, Sanchez C. Protein–polysaccharide interactions. Current opinion in Colloid & interface Science. 2000 Jul 1;5(3-4):202-214.

[131] Burger TG, Zhang Y. Recent progress in the utilization of pea protein as an emulsifier for food applications. Trends in Food Science & Technology. 2019 Apr 1;86:25-33.

[132] Tang CH. Emulsifying properties of soy proteins: A critical review with emphasis on the role of conformational flexibility. Critical Reviews in Food Science and Nutrition. 2017 Aug 13;57(12):2636-2679.

[133] Jeske S, Zannini E, Arendt EK. Past, present and future: The strength of plant-based dairy substitutes based on gluten-free raw materials. Food research international. 2018 Aug 1;110:42-51.

[134] Karaca AC, Low N, Nickerson M. Emulsifying properties of chickpea, faba bean, lentil and pea proteins produced by isoelectric precipitation and salt extraction. Food Research International. 2011 Nov 1;44(9):2742-2750.

[135] Gumus CE, Decker EA, McClements DJ. Formation and stability of ω-3 oil emulsion-based delivery systems using plant proteins as emulsifiers: Lentil, pea, and faba bean proteins. Food Biophysics. 2017 Jun 1;12(2):186-197.

[136] Ozturk B, Argin S, Ozilgen M, McClements DJ. Formation and stabilization of nanoemulsion-based vitamin E delivery systems using natural biopolymers: Whey protein isolate and gum arabic. Food Chemistry. 2015 Dec 1;188:256-263.

[137] Xu Y, Wang C, Fu X, Huang Q, Zhang B. Effect of pH and ionic strength on the emulsifying properties of two Octenylsuccinate starches in comparison with gum Arabic. Food Hydrocolloids. 2018 Mar 1;76:96-102.

[138] Euston SR. Computer simulation of proteins: adsorption, gelation and self-association. Current opinion in colloid & interface science. 2004 Dec 1;9(5):321-327.

[139] McClements DJ, Newman E, McClements IF. Plant-based Milks: A Review of the Science Underpinning Their Design, Fabrication, and Performance. Comprehensive Reviews in Food Science and Food Safety. 2019 Nov;18(6):2047-2067.

[140] Bals A, Kulozik U. Effect of pre-heating on the foaming properties of whey protein isolate using a membrane foaming apparatus. International Dairy Journal. 2003 Jan 1;13(11):903-908.

[141] Mitidieri FE, Wagner JR. Coalescence of o/w emulsions stabilized by whey and isolate soybean proteins. Influence of thermal denaturation, salt addition and competitive interfacial adsorption. Food Research International. 2002 Jan 1;35(6):547-557.

[142] Kato AK. Industrial applications of Maillard-type protein-polysaccharide conjugates. Food Science and Technology Research. 2002;8(3):193-199.

[143] Schwenke KD. Enzyme and chemical modification. Food proteins and their applications, Damodaran S., Paraf A.(Hrsg.), Marcel Dekker, New York. 1997 Mar 12:393-423.

[144] Damodaran S. Amino acids, peptides, and proteins. In: Fennema OR, editor. Food chemistry. New York: Marcel Dekker. 1996:p:321-429.

[145] Liu M, Damodaran S. Effect of transglutaminase-catalyzed polymerization of β-casein on its emulsifying properties. Journal of Agricultural and Food Chemistry. 1999 Apr 19;47(4):1514-1519.

[146] El Fadil EB, Khan MA, Matsudomi N, Kato A. Polymerization of soy protein digests by microbial transglutaminase for improvement of the functional properties. Food research international. 1996 Oct 1;29(7):627-634.

[147] Dickinson E. Hydrocolloids at interfaces and the influence on the properties of dispersed systems. Food hydrocolloids. 2003 Jan 1;17(1):25-39.

[148] Leroux J, Langendorff V, Schick G, Vaishnav V, Mazoyer J. Emulsion stabilizing properties of pectin. Food Hydrocolloids. 2003 Jul 1;17(4):455-462.

[149] Parker A, Gunning PA, Ng K, Robins MM. How does xanthan stabilise salad dressing?. Food Hydrocolloids. 1995 Dec 1;9(4):333-342.

[150] Güzey D, McClements DJ. Influence of environmental stresses on O/W emulsions stabilized by β-lactoglobulin–pectin and β-lactoglobulin–pectin–chitosan membranes produced by the electrostatic layer-by-layer deposition technique. Food Biophysics. 2006 Mar 1;1(1):30-40.

[151] De Gennes PG. Polymers at an interface; a simplified view. Advances in colloid and interface science. 1987 Jul 1;27(3-4):189-209.

[152] Dickinson E, Flint FO, Hunt JA. Bridging flocculation in binary protein stabilized emulsions. Food Hydrocolloids. 1989 Nov 1;3(5):389-397.

[153] Syrbe A, Bauer WJ, Klostermeyer HJ. Polymer science concepts in dairy systems—an overview of milk protein and food hydrocolloid interaction. International dairy journal. 1998 Mar 1;8(3):179-193.

[154] Asakura S, Oosawa F. On interaction between two bodies immersed in a solution of macromolecules. The Journal of chemical physics. 1954 Jul;22(7):1255-1256.

[155] Asakura S, Oosawa F. Interaction between particles suspended in solutions of macromolecules. Journal of polymer science. 1958 Dec;33(126):183-192.

[156] Dickinson E. Emulsion stabilization by polysaccharides and protein-polysaccharide complexes. Food Science and Technology-New York-MarceL Dekker. 1995:501-515.

[157] Warren PB. Phase behavior of a colloid+ binary polymer mixture: theory. Langmuir. 1997 Aug 20;13(17):4588-4594.

[158] McClements DJ. Food emulsions: principles, practice and techniques. Boca Raton, Fla: CRC Press. 1999.

[159] Munekata PE, Domínguez R, Budaraju S, Roselló-Soto E, Barba FJ, Mallikarjunan K, Roohinejad S, Lorenzo JM. Effect of innovative food processing technologies on the

physicochemical and nutritional properties and quality of non-dairy plant-based beverages. Foods. 2020 Mar;9(3):288.

[160] Cruz N, Capellas M, Hernández M, Trujillo AJ, Guamis B, Ferragut V. Ultra high pressure homogenization of soymilk: Microbiological, physicochemical and microstructural characteristics. Food Research International. 2007 Jul 1;40(6):725-732.

[161] Valencia-Flores DC, Hernández-Herrero M, Guamis B, Ferragut V. Comparing the effects of ultra-high-pressure homogenization and conventional thermal treatments on the microbiological, physical, and chemical quality of almond beverages. Journal of Food Science. 2013 Feb;78(2):E199–E205.

[162] Poliseli-Scopel FH, Hernández-Herrero M, Guamis B, Ferragut V. Sterilization and aseptic packaging of soymilk treated by ultra high pressure homogenization. Innovative Food Science & Emerging Technologies. 2014 Apr 1;22:81-88.

[163] Barba FJ, Parniakov O, Pereira SA, Wiktor A, Grimi N, Boussetta N, Saraiva JA, Raso J, Martin-Belloso O, Witrowa-Rajchert D, Lebovka N. Current applications and new opportunities for the use of pulsed electric fields in food science and industry. Food Research International. 2015 Nov 1;77:773-798.

[164] Xiang BY. *Effects of pulsed electric fields on structural modification and rheological properties for selected food proteins* (Doctoral dissertation, McGill University).

[165] Cortés C, Esteve MJ, Frıgola A, Torregrosa F. Quality characteristics of horchata (a Spanish vegetable beverage) treated with pulsed electric fields during shelf-life. Food Chemistry. 2005 Jun 1;91(2):319-325.

[166] Iswarin SJ, Permadi B. Coconut milk's fat breaking by means of ultrasound. International Journal of Basic & Applied Sciences. 2012;12(1):1-5.

Chapter 4

Kenaf (*Hibiscus cannabinus* L.) Seed Extract as a New Plant-Based Milk Alternative and Its Potential Food Uses

Roselina Karim, Nor Aini Mat Noh, Shafa'atu Giwa Ibrahim, Wan Zunairah Wan Ibadullah, Norhasnida Zawawi and Nazamid Saari

Abstract

Kenaf (*Hibiscus cannabinus* L.) seed is rich in protein, fat, fiber, and other essential nutrients. Kenaf seed comprises of high protein (22–31%) and oil (22–25%) contents which suggested its high potential food application. This chapter discusses the potential and early development of kenaf-based plant-milk and tofu. The step-by-step processes involved in preparation of kenaf-based milk and kenaf-based tofu at laboratory-scale are illustrated. Soaking conditions (temperature and time) of kenaf seed as pretreatment in preparation of kenaf seed milk were highlighted. Hydration of kenaf seed were found to be faster at elevated temperature, however higher soaking temperature and prolonged soaking time causes some losses of protein (%) and solid content (%) which are unfavorable for production of highly nutritious plant-based milk. Furthermore, in preparation of kenaf-based tofu, soaking temperature of seed also affected the properties of the tofu. As the soaking temperature was increased from 25–65°C, the yield, hardness, and chewiness of kenaf tofu decreased. It was recommended that soaking of kenaf seed at 25°C and the use of aluminum potassium salt at 1.00 g% as coagulant produces kenaf-based tofu with optimum quality.

Keywords: kenaf seed, soaking temperature, milky extract, hydration, physicochemical quality, chemical composition, kenaf-based tofu

1. Introduction

Kenaf (*Hibiscus cannabinus* L.) is one of the most important fiber crops, belonging to the family of Malvaceae. Kenaf is cultivated in more than 20 countries where it is widely grown in China, India, and Thailand [1]. Kenaf is a useful multi-purpose crop with various industrial applications from paper to furniture and from biofuel to textile. Besides being a cordage crop it has substantial role in the construction and automotive industry. Kenaf plant has a significant economic value since all parts of the plant including the stem, leaves, flowers, and seeds can be used to the full advantage for mankind. In the recent years, considerable attention and research has been carried out on the potential application of kenaf seeds in the food industry. Kenaf seed is reported as rich in fat, protein, dietary fibers, and a good source of raw material for production of edible oil, flour, protein concentrate, as well as potential ingredient for nutraceuticals and functional foods [2–4].

2. Chemical composition

The proximate composition of different varieties of kenaf seed is presented in **Table 1**. The kenaf seed cultivars QP3, V36, and KB6 were cultivated in Malaysia while the seed cultivar C14 was cultivated in Korea, originated from Italy [2, 5, 6]. The seed varieties possess different chemical composition due to variation in agronomic conditions such as soil type, environmental variation, agriculture input (such as fertilizer application), planting season, maturity stage, harvesting period, and post-harvest treatments such as drying and storage conditions [2]. In general, kenaf seed is high in protein and fat content which comprises of 21.9–30.5% and 22.1–24.8%, respectively. Kenaf seed was also reported to have a considerable amount of carbohydrate (18.7–24.4%) and fibers (10.6–18.7%).

The fatty acid composition of kenaf milk was not affected by processing. Both the kenaf seed and the milk contain high concentration of hexadecanoic acid (palmitic acid), 9-octadecenoic acid (oleic acid) and 9,12-octadecadienoic acid (linoleic acid) (**Table 2**). These saturated and unsaturated fatty acids had been reported as the major fatty acids in other kenaf seed cultivars [7–9]. The kenaf seed and its milk were not significantly different in their saturated, mono- and poly-unsaturated fatty acids composition. Based on the 9-octadecenoic and 9,12-octadecadienoic acid contents, the oil from the kenaf seed and kenaf milk are less prone to rancidity and might be used as edible healthier oils. Oleic acid is suggested to show a protective effect on Alzheimer's disease and other neurological disorders. A study on mouse model supplemented with oleic acid and restricted cholesterol intake had reduced the Alzheimer's disease-type neuropathology [10]. Linoleic acid plays an important role in reducing the total cholesterol level. It was found that the presence of high linoleic acid (33.6%) in kenaf seed extract exhibited an anti-hypercholesterolemic effect [11]. The presence of these beneficial bioactive compounds suggested the potential nutraceutical properties of the kenaf seed and kenaf seed milk.

The amino acid profile of kenaf seed has not been well studied. The non-essential amino acids composition of kenaf seed were significantly higher than the kenaf milk except for the proline content (**Table 3**). Also, kenaf seed was significantly higher

Composition (%)	Kenaf QP3	Kenaf V36	Kenaf KB6	Kenaf C14
Moisture	8.5	8.4	9.0	8.3
Crude protein[A]	30.5	29.8	21.9	27.5
Crude fat	24.8	22.6	24.7	22.1
Crude fiber	12.5	11.5	18.7	10.6
Ash	4.5	4.5	6.2	5.8
Total carbohydrate[B]	19.2	23.2	18.7	24.4

[A]*Crude protein = N (%) × 6.25.*
[B]*By difference.*

Table 1.
Proximate composition of several kenaf seed varieties [2, 5, 6].

Chemical name	Molecular formula	Kenaf seed area (%)	Kenaf milk area (%)
Methyl tetradecanoate (15:0)	$C_{15}H_{30}O_2$	0.03 ± 0.01[b]	0.05 ± 0.01[a]
Hexadecanoic acid (16:0)	$C_{16}H_{32}O_2$	26.71 ± 0.22[a]	26.11 ± 0.57[a]
9-Hexadecenoic acid (16:1)	$C_{16}H_{30}O_2$	0.40 ± 0.02[a]	0.28 ± 0.01[b]
Heptadecanoic acid (17:0)	$C_{17}H_{34}O_2$	0.04 ± 0.00[b]	0.05 ± 0.00[a]
Octadecanoic acid (18:0)	$C_{18}H_{36}O_2$	3.17 ± 0.47[a]	2.94 ± 0.05[a]
9-Octadecenoic acid (18:1)	$C_{18}H_{34}O_2$	33.80 ± 2.39[a]	40.41 ± 1.22[a]
9,12-Octadecadienoic acid (18:2)	$C_{18}H_{32}O_2$	30.59 ± 0.62[a]	28.62 ± 0.86[a]
10-Nonadecenoic acid (20:1)	$C_{20}H_{38}O_2$	0.55 ± 0.04[b]	0.74 ± 0.01[a]
Methyl 18-methylnonadecanoate (21:0)	$C_{21}H_{42}O_2$	0.31 ± 0.01[a]	0.46 ± 0.18[a]
Docosanoic acid (22:0)	$C_{22}H_{44}O_2$	0.15 ± 0.01[a]	0.19 ± 0.01[a]
Tetracosanoic acid (24:0)	$C_{24}H_{48}O_2$	0.10 ± 0.01[a]	0.13 ± 0.02[a]
Saturated		30.51 ± 0.73[a]	29.93 ± 0.84[a]
Monounsaturated		34.75 ± 2.45[a]	41.12 ± 1.24[a]
Polyunsaturated		30.59 ± 0.62[a]	28.62 ± 0.86[a]

The values within the same row with different superscripts letters are significantly different at $P \leq 0.05$.

Table 2.
Composition and amount (%) of saturated and unsaturated fatty acids of kenaf seed KB6 variety.

Amino acids	Kenaf seed (mg/g)	Kenaf seed milk (mg/g)
Asp	114.39 ± 4.29[a]	94.21 ± 0.01[a]
Ser	87.97 ± 5.92[a]	35.14 ± 0.01[b]
Glu	124.37 ± 2.87[a]	58.77 ± 0.01[c]
Arg	178.72 ± 0.89[a]	70.79 ± 1.61[b]
Gly	62.21 ± 2.25[a]	23.79 ± 0.01[b]
Ala	46.61 ± 4.33[a]	14.70 ± 0.01[b]
Pro	35.69 ± 2.75[b]	54.31 ± 0.01[a]
Tyr	34.15 ± 0.46[a]	11.04 ± 0.00[b]
Non-essential	684.11[a]	362.75[b]
His	39.67 ± 2.35[a]	17.79 ± 0.01[b]
Thr	54.65 ± 2.31[a]	19.14 ± 0.01[b]
Lys	59.87 ± 1.47[b]	56.81 ± 0.02[b]
Val	64.11 ± 2.14[a]	28.24 ± 0.01[c]
Met	28.09 ± 0.79[a]	12.00 ± 0.00[b]
Ile	54.07 ± 0.36[b]	95.50 ± 1.35[a]
Leu	91.32 ± 0.62[b]	129.59 ± 0.04[a]
Phe	71.01 ± 0.51[b]	128.34 ± 0.04[a]
Essential	462.79[a]	487.41[a]

The values within the same row with different superscripts letters are significantly different at $P \leq 0.05$.

Table 3.
Amino acid profiles of KB6 kenaf seed and kenaf seed milk.

than the milk in terms of the essential amino acids such as histidine, threonine, valine and methionine. These indicated that the processes of extraction of the kenaf milk affected the amino acid content of the milk. However, the total essential amino acids of the seed and the milk were not significantly different.

3. Seed hydration

Soaking is commonly used in processing of grains, to soften and hydrate the seed before proceeding to other stages such as cooking, extraction, fermentation, germination and malting [12]. In preparation of a plant-based milk alternative, an initial soaking of the plant seed is a prerequisite before extraction of the milk constituent by wet milling. Soaking of seeds reduced the hard-to-cook nature by softening the texture of the seeds which in turn facilitates subsequent processes and reduces the cooking time. Soaking is a batch process which can take an average

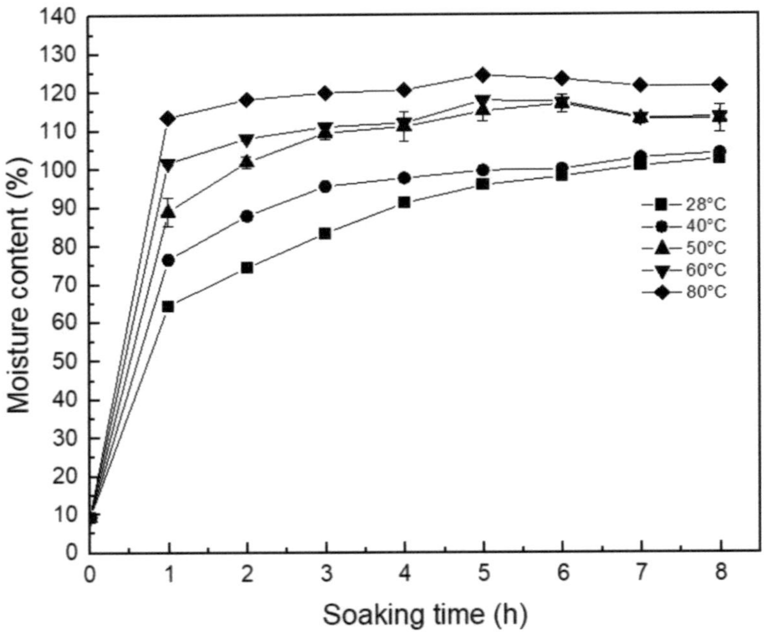

Figure 1.
Moisture content (%) (d.b.) of kenaf seed soaked at different time and temperature.

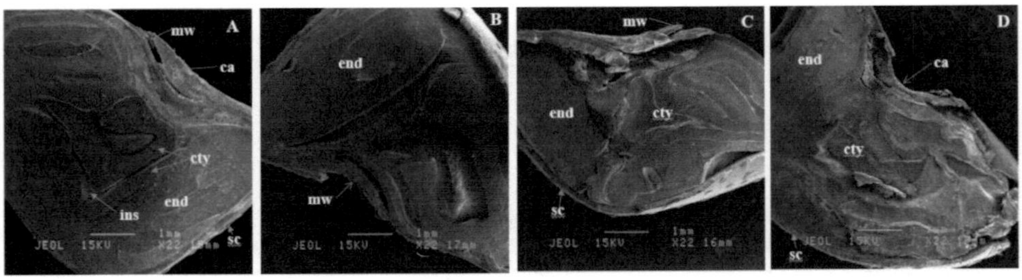

Figure 2.
Effect of soaking temperatures on the scanning electron microscopy images of kenaf seeds. Note: A = unsoaked kenaf seed, B = kenaf seed soaked at 25°C, C = kenaf seed soaked at 45°C, D = kenaf seed soaked at 65°C, mw = major entrance of water, ca = caruncle, cty = cotyledon, end = endosperm, sc = seed coat, ins = intracellular spaces (adapted from [5]).

of 12 to 24 h at room temperature (25 + 2°C) and uses a substantial quantity of water. However, numerous ways to accelerate the process have been proposed which include soaking at elevated temperatures, high-power ultrasound, and high hydrostatic pressure [13].

Hydration at higher temperature is one of the most frequently used techniques in enhancing the hydration rate of plant seeds. **Figure 1** shows the water absorption rate of kenaf seed as a function of soaking temperature and time (unpublished data). It was observed that the highest water absorption rate of kenaf seed was recorded at the highest soaking temperature (80°C). Higher soaking temperature causes reduction in the soaking medium viscosity which improves the capillary flow and dilatation of the tissues and pores, hence increases the water absorption rate [14]. At the beginning of soaking, water absorption rate was high, and it gradually slowed down towards the end of soaking process. The former action was due to the predominant of capillarity flow of seed hydration mechanism while the latter was due to diffusion process [13]. The effectiveness of using higher temperature in increasing the absorption rate was also reported in other studies [15–18]. Further investigation on the effect of kenaf seed hydration towards its microstructure was studied using the scanning electron microscopy and is presented in **Figure 2**. It was observed that kenaf seed soaked at 25°C (**Figure 2B**) had a more visible intracellular spaces than the seed soaked at 45°C (**Figure 2C**), and 65°C (**Figure 2D**). The intracellular spaces inside the seeds soaked at 45°C and 65°C were filled with water and both the endosperm and cotyledon segment appeared expanded. Therefore, it is evident that hydration rate of seed soaked at higher temperature increased and causes further improvement in the capillarity flow and dilatation of the tissues and pores of kenaf seed.

4. Effect of soaking condition on nutritional quality of kenaf seed milky extract

Although the use of high soaking temperature acts as a steeping factor for the soaking process, it generates a notable loss of solids from seeds such as protein (%) and solid content (%). Therefore, in preparation of kenaf seed milk, selection of suitable soaking conditions (temperature and time) need to be considered in minimizing the solid loss during soaking process.

Figures 3 and **4** show the effect of soaking temperature towards the subsequent protein content (%) and solid content (%) (expressed in °Brix) of the kenaf seed milky extract, respectively (unpublished data). From **Figure 3**, the protein content of kenaf seed milky extract were found to be increased with prolonged soaking time at lower soaking temperatures (28°C and 40°C) and decreased throughout the soaking period after the first hour of soaking at higher temperature (50°C, 60°C, 80°C). This result may be due to the release of some seed component including proteins into the soaking medium which is enhanced by the higher soaking temperature and time. Soaking at higher temperature causes the loose of seed coat structure and thus the seed storage proteins (7S and 11S proteins) that are protected by the seed coat were released into the soaking medium by the force of concentration difference [19]. Other than proteins, the leaching of the seed component may include carbohydrates [20]. The release of soluble solids from the seed were found to increase at higher soaking temperature due to the extended seed wall rupture. Based on **Figure 4**, the solid content of kenaf seed milky extract increased with longer soaking time of kenaf seed at lower temperatures (28°C and 40°C), and decreased at higher temperature (50°C, 60°C, 80°C) of soaking. The increased of solid loss upon higher temperature of soaking were also reported by other researchers [18, 20, 21].

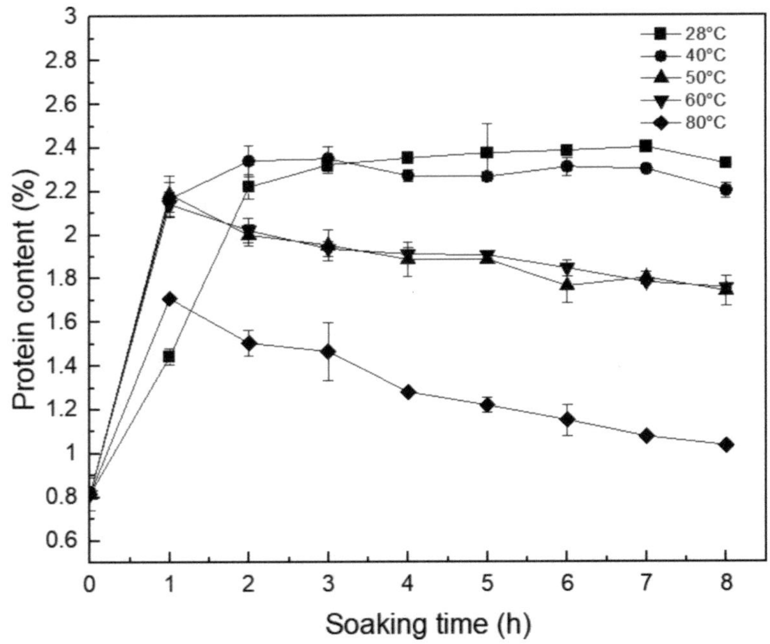

Figure 3.
Protein content (%) of kenaf seed milky extract obtained from different soaking condition (time and temperature) of kenaf seed.

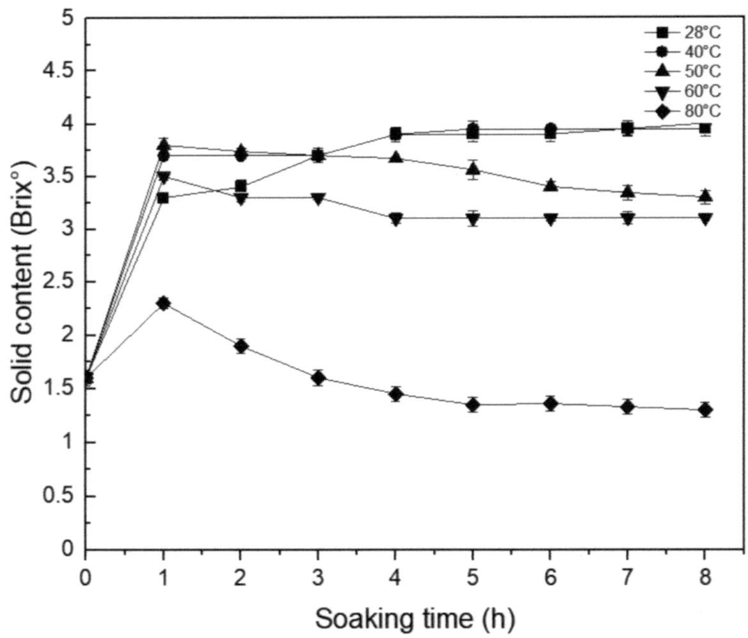

Figure 4.
Solid content (°brix) of kenaf seed milky extract obtained using different soaking condition (time and temperature) of kenaf seed.

5. Kenaf seed milk

Figure 5 shows the procedures for the preparation of kenaf seed milk. Kenaf seed milk appears to be similar in appearance and texture to soymilk with creamy

Figure 5.
Processes in preparation of kenaf seed milk.

Compositions	Kenaf seed milk	Soymilk [22, 23]	Almond milk [22, 23]	Hemp milk [24, 25]
Moisture (%)	91.04	88.12–91.00	72.00–93.40	91.60
Protein (%)	1.93–2.48	3.82–3.98	1.90–2.50	0.83–4.00
Fat content (%)	2.10–2.60	3.10–4.30	3.20–3.60	1.25–3.00
Carbohydrate (%)	1.82	4.64–4.92	4.30–4.70	2.50–20.00
Ash content (%)	3.11	0.84–0.81	0.09–3.04	0.47

Table 4.
The proximate composition of kenaf seed milk (seed variety V36) and several commercially available plant-based milk alternatives.

white in color. The taste of the unflavored kenaf seed milk is described as thin with a hint of earthy flavor. **Table 4** shows the proximate composition of kenaf milk in comparison to several commercially available plant-based milk alternatives. Kenaf seed milk contains 1.93–2.48% of protein and 2.10–2.60% fat which is comparable to almond milk in terms of the protein and fat contents, respectively.

6. Processing of value-added kenaf based tofu derived from kenaf seed milk

Tofu is a popular and important protein source in most countries such as Asian, Western and African countries [26, 27]. Over the years, soybean has been the most commonly used legume for tofu production. However, several researchers have produced tofu from other grains such as peanut [28], lupin seed [29], sesame [30], chickpea and mung bean [31]; in most cases the selection of these grains were based on their high protein content and good functional properties. Kenaf seed have been reported to contain 21.4 to 30.5% protein on dry basis [6, 32] and protein has been known as one of the factors that affect tofu quality [29, 33, 34]. The general processing of soybean tofu involves soaking of the seed, grinding with water, boiling of the slurry, followed by separation of the milk from the residue (kenaf seed okara), cooking of the milk to 95°C, coagulating the cooked milk and molding [35]. Recently, we have produced kenaf-based tofu from kenaf seed milk and the effect of processing variables such as soaking temperature of kenaf seed, coagulant types and concentrations were investigated [5]. The outcomes of our research indicated that the yield, hardness, and chewiness of the kenaf-based tofu decreased as the soaking temperature increased from 25–65°C. Besides, the interaction among the processing variables such as coagulant type*coagulant concentration, coagulant type*soaking temperature and coagulant concentrations*soaking temperature affected the yield, hardness, and chewiness of the kenaf-based tofu (**Figure 6**). It was discovered that soaking of kenaf seed at 25°C and using aluminum potassium salt as coagulant at concentration of 1.00 g% were recommended as the processing variables for optimum kenaf-based tofu production.

The procedure for kenaf-based tofu preparation slightly differs from the processing for soybean tofu whereby the kenaf seed slurry is not heated prior to extraction. Additionally, 1:5 to 1:8 soybean-to-water ratios were often used in the extraction of soybean milk for tofu production. However, in the case of kenaf-based

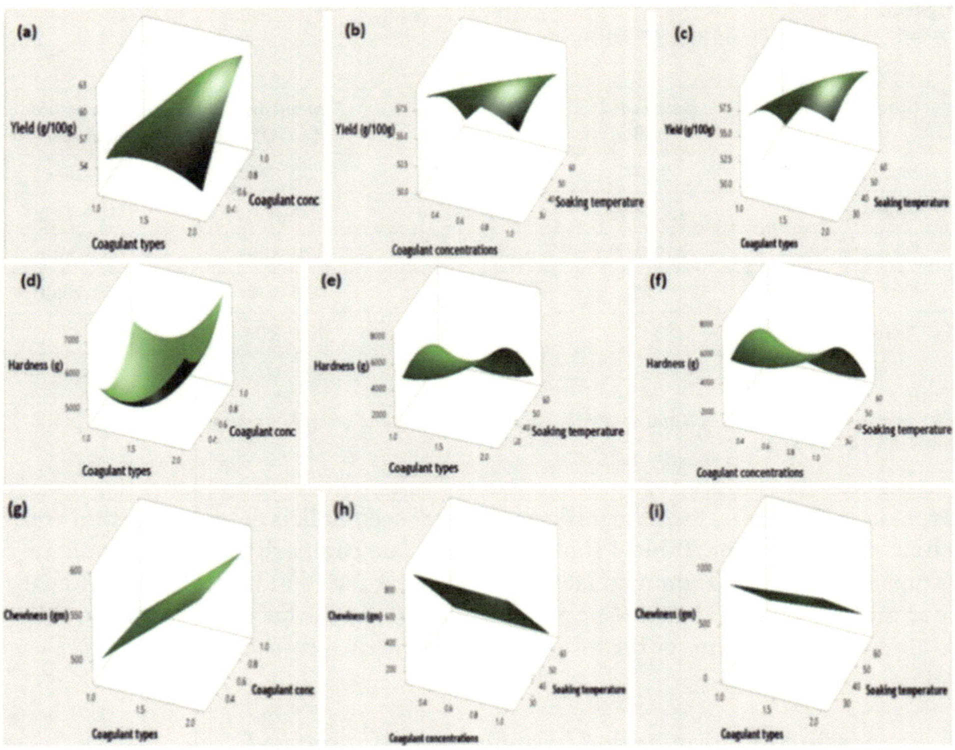

Figure 6.
Surface plots of interactions of coagulant types, coagulant concentrations, and soaking temperature of seed on yield, hardness, and chewiness of kenaf-based tofu. Note: a, b, c = surface plots of yield; d, e, f = surface plots of hardness; g, h, i = surface plots of chewiness (adapted from [5]).

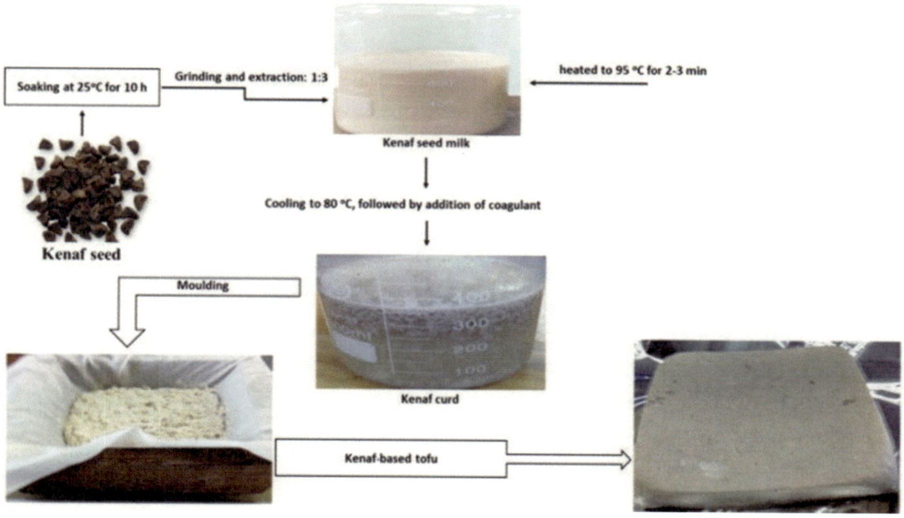

Figure 7.
Procedures for production of kenaf seed tofu (adapted from [5]).

tofu it was discovered that the most suitable ratio of kenaf seed to water for the extraction of the milk during tofu production was 1:3, based on the lower total soluble solids content of kenaf milk (unpublished data). The procedure for the production of kenaf-based tofu is presented in **Figure 7**, the kenaf seed was soaked at 25°C for 10 h and the soaked seed was ground at low speed using 1:3 kenaf seed-to-water ratio for 2–3 min. The slurry obtained was then filtered using muslin cloth to separate the kenaf seed residue from the milk. The milk obtained (400 ml) from 100 g of kenaf seed was heated until the temperature of the milk reached 95°C and the temperature was hold at this temperature for 2–3 min. Then, the milk was allowed to cool to 80°C at room temperature (25 ± 2°C) and the specified coagulant was added to form the kenaf seed curd. The curd was then transferred to a wooden mold lined with muslin cloth and pressed with a load of 5 kg for 5 min to remove excess water. A solid curd-like product known as kenaf seed tofu is formed and is ready to be used or consumed.

7. Other potential uses of kenaf seed

Several other potential food applications of kenaf seed have been postulated based on the functional characteristics of its protein concentrate [36]. The authors have proposed the use of kenaf seed as an ingredient in the production of vegetable-based protein substitute such as tempeh and texturized vegetable protein. Tempeh is a fermented vegetable meat substitute produced by inoculating pre-cooked legumes such as soybean, lentils and common bean with *Rhizopus oligosporus* [37, 38]. Similarly, pre-cooked kenaf seed can be fermented with *Rhizopus oligosporus* to produce kenaf-based tempeh based on its high protein content and emulsifying property (unpublished data). Additionally, kenaf seed protein concentrate has been reported to have high thermal stability [2]. Thus, protein concentrate from kenaf seed can be extruded into slices, crumbles, flakes and chunks to produce a meat-like chewy texture similar to texturized soy protein [39]. Also, kenaf seed has been used in the form of defatted meal or flour for the production of noodles and pasta [40].

8. Conclusion

Kenaf seed is a highly nutritious plant seed that should be further exploited in innovation of non-conventional plant-based milk alternative and other food uses. In this chapter, the soaking conditions (temperature and time) of kenaf seed were studied. Higher soaking temperature and prolonged soaking time of kenaf seed were not recommended as they caused the loss of protein (%) and soluble solids (%) of the seed milky extract. Higher soaking temperature was also found to reduce the physical properties (yield, hardness, and chewiness) of kenaf-based tofu. It is recommended to use a lower temperature (25°C and 40°C) of soaking to preserve the nutritional value and quality of the subsequent products. Further and more thorough research ought to be done to produce a highly nutritious and highest quality of plant-based milk and tofu from kenaf seed that are comparable to the established soymilk and soy tofu, respectively.

Acknowledgements

This research was supported and funded by the National Kenaf and Tobacco Board of Malaysia (Vote No.:6300910-UPM), Tertiary Education Trust Fund (TETFund) and Usmanu Danfodiyo University, Sokoto (UDUS).

Author details

Roselina Karim[1*], Nor Aini Mat Noh[1], Shafa'atu Giwa Ibrahim[1,2], Wan Zunairah Wan Ibadullah[3], Norhasnida Zawawi[3] and Nazamid Saari[3]

1 Department of Food Technology, Faculty of Food Science and Technology, Universiti Putra Malaysia, Serdang, Selangor, Malaysia

2 Department of Biochemistry, Faculty of Science, Usmanu Danfodiyo University, Sokoto, Nigeria

3 Department of Food Science, Faculty of Food Science and Technology, Universiti Putra Malaysia, Serdang, Selangor, Malaysia

*Address all correspondence to: rosaz@upm.edu.my

References

[1] Cheng W-Y, Haque Akanda JM, Nyam K-L. Kenaf seed oil: A potential new source of edible oil. Trends in Food Science and Technology [Internet]. 2016 Jun 1 [cited 2020 Mar 13];52:57-65. Available from: https://www.sciencedirect.com/science/article/pii/S0924224415301242?via%3Dihub

[2] Mariod AA, Fathy SF, Ismail M. Preparation and characterisation of protein concentrates from defatted kenaf seed. Food Chemistry [Internet]. 2010;123(3):747-52. Available from: http://dx.doi.org/10.1016/j.foodchem.2010.05.045

[3] Chan KW, Khong NMH, Iqbal S, Mansor SM, Ismail M. Defatted kenaf seed meal (DKSM): Prospective edible flour from agricultural waste with high antioxidant activity. LWT - Food Sci Technol [Internet]. 2013;53(1):308-13. Available from: http://dx.doi.org/10.1016/j.lwt.2013.01.003

[4] Dhar P, Kar CS, Ojha D, Pandey SK, Mitra J. Chemistry, phytotechnology, pharmacology and nutraceutical functions of kenaf (Hibiscus cannabinus L.) and roselle (Hibiscus sabdariffa L.) seed oil: An overview. Industrial Crops and Products [Internet]. 2015;77:323-32. Available from: http://dx.doi.org/10.1016/j.indcrop.2015.08.064

[5] Ibrahim G, Mat Noh NA, Wan Ibadullah WZ, Saari N, Karim R. Water soaking temperature of kenaf (Hibiscus cannabinus L.) seed, coagulant types, and their concentrations affected the production of kenaf-based tofu. Journal of Food Processing & Preservation. November 2019;**2020**:1-13

[6] Kim D, Ryu J, Lee M, Kim JM, Ahn J, Kim J, et al. Nutritional properties of various tissues from new kenaf cultivars. J Crop Sci Biotech. 2018;**21**(3):229-239

[7] Nyam KL, Tan CP, Lai OM, Long K, Man YBC. Physicochemical properties and bioactive compounds of selected seed oils. LWT - Food Sci Technol. 2009;**42**(8):1396-1403

[8] Mohamed A, Bhardwaj H, Hamama A, Webber C. Chemical composition of kenaf (Hibiscus cannabinus L.) seed oil. Industrial Crops and Products. 1995;**4**(3):157-165

[9] Chew SC, Tan CP, Long K, Nyam KL. Effect of chemical refining on the quality of kenaf (Hibiscus cannabinus) seed oil. Industrial Crops and Products. 2016;**89**:59-65

[10] Amtul Z, Westaway D, Cechetto DF, Rozmahel RF. Oleic acid ameliorates amyloidosis in cellular and mouse models of Alzheimer's disease. Brain Pathology. 2011;**21**(2):321-329

[11] Kai NS, Nee TA, Lai E, Ling C, Ping TC, Kamariah L, et al. Anti-hypercholesterolemic effect of kenaf (Hibiscus cannabinus L.) seed on high-fat diet Sprague Dawley rats. Asian Pac J Trop Med [Internet]. 2015;8(1):6-13. Available from: http://dx.doi.org/10.1016/S1995-7645(14)60179-6

[12] Deshpande SS, Sathe SK, Salunkhe DK. Soaking. In: Salunkhe DK, Kadam SS, editors. CRC Handbook of World Food Legumes: Nutritional Chemistry, Processing Technology, and Utilization. Boca Raton, Florida: CRC Press, Inc.; 1989. p. 133-40.

[13] Miano AC, Augusto PED. The hydration of grains: A critical review from description of phenomena to process improvements. Comprehensive Reviews in Food Science and Food Safety. 2018;**17**(2):352-370

[14] Oliveira AL, Colnaghi BG, Zucatti E, Gouvêa IR, Vieira RL, Esteves P, et al. Modelling the effect of

temperature on the hydration kinetic of adzuki beans (Vigna angularis). Journal of Food Engineering [Internet]. 2013;118(4):417-20. Available from: http://dx.doi.org/10.1016/j.jfoodeng.2013.04.034

[15] Shafaei SM, Masoumi AA, Roshan H. Analysis of water absorption of bean and chickpea during soaking using Peleg model. Journal of the Saudi Society of Agricultural Sciences [Internet]. 2016;15(2):135-44. Available from: http://dx.doi.org/10.1016/j.jssas.2014.08.003

[16] Johnny S, Razavi SM, Khodaei D. Hydration kinetics and physical properties of split chickpea as affected by soaking temperature and time. Journal of Food Science and Technology. 2015;**52**(12):8377-8382

[17] Quicazán MC, Caicedo LA, Cuenca M. Applying Peleg's equation to modelling the kinetics of solid hydration and migration during soybean soaking. Ing e Investig. 2012;**32**(3):53-57

[18] Khazaei J, Mohammadi N. Effect of temperature on hydration kinetics of sesame seeds (Sesamum indicum L.). Journal of Food Engineering [Internet]. 2009;91(4):542-52. Available from: http://dx.doi.org/10.1016/j.jfoodeng.2008.10.010

[19] Li X, Liu X, Hua Y, Chen Y, Kong X, Zhang C. Effects of water absorption of soybean seed on the quality of soymilk and the release of flavor compounds. RSC Advances. 2019;**9**(6):2906-2918

[20] Pan Z, Tangratanavalee W. Characteristics of soybeans as affected by soaking conditions. LWT - Food Sci Technol. 2003;**36**(1):143-151

[21] Lima FS De, Kurozawa LE, Ida EI. The effects of soybean soaking on grain properties and isoflavones loss. LWT - Food Sci Technol [Internet]. 2014;59(2):1274-82. Available from: http://dx.doi.org/10.1016/j.lwt.2014.04.032

[22] Kundu P, Dhankhar J, Sharma A. Development of non dairy milk alternative using soymilk and almond milk. Curr Res Nutr Food Sci. 2018;**06**(1):203-210

[23] Alozie YE, Udofia US. Nutritional and sensory properties of almond (Prunus amygdalu var. Dulcis) seed milk. World Journal of Dairy & Food Sciences. 2015;**10**(2):117-121

[24] Chich owska J, Kliber A, Biskupski M, Grygorowicz Z. Insulin, thyroid hormone levels and metabolic changes after treated rats with hemp milk. 2002; Available from: https://pdfs.semanticscholar.org/2625/168857ebe1cf4bfb987532dcc278c2d92eb5.pdf

[25] USDA. United States Department of Agriculture food composition database [Internet]. [cited 2020 Sep 8]. Available from: https://ndb.nal.usda.gov/

[26] Zhu Q, Wu F, Saito M, Tatsumi E, Yin L. Effect of magnesium salt concentration in water-in-oil emulsions on the physical properties and microstructure of tofu. Food Chemistry. 2016;**201**:197-204

[27] Oboh G. Coagulants modulate the hypocholesterolemic effect of tofu (coagulated soymilk). African J Biotechnol. 2006;**5**(3):290-294

[28] Guo Y, Hu H, Wang Q, Liu H. A novel process for peanut tofu gel: Its texture, microstructure and protein behavioral changes affected by processing conditions. LWT - Food Sci Technol. 2018;**96**:140-146

[29] Jayasena V, Khu WS, Nasar-Abbas SM. The development and sensory acceptability of lupin-based

tofu. Journal of Food Quality. 2010;**33**(1):85-97

[30] Sato E. Effects of different kind of sesame materials on the physical properties of gomatofu (sesame tofu). Food Hydrocolloids. 2003;**17**(6):901-906

[31] Mohamed S, Johan Z, Chickpea BJ. Mungbean, cowpea and peanuts as substitutes for soybean curds. International Journal of Food Science and Technology. 1989;**24**(4):385-394

[32] Olawepo KD, Banjo OT, Jimoh WA, Fawole WO, Orisasona O, Ojo-Daniel AH. Effect of cooking and roasting on nutritional and anti-nutritional factors in kenaf (Hibiscus cannabinus L.) seed meal. Food Sci Qual Manag. 2014;**24**:2224-6088

[33] Mujoo R, Trinh DT, Ng PK. Characterization of storage proteins in different soybean varieties and their relationship to tofu yield and texture. Food Chemistry. 2003;**82**(2):265-273

[34] Evans DE, Tsukamoto C, Nielsen NC. A small scale method for the production of soymilk and silken tofu. Crop Science. 1997;**37**(5):1463-1471

[35] Cao FH, Li XJ, Luo SZ, Mu DD, Zhong XY, Jiang ST, et al. Effects of organic acid coagulants on the physical properties of and chemical interactions in tofu. LWT - Food Sci Technol. 2017;**85**:58-65

[36] Giwa Ibrahim S, Karim R, Saari N, Wan Abdullah WZ, Zawawi N, Ab Razak AF, et al. Kenaf (Hibiscus cannabinus L.) seed and its potential food applications: A review. Journal of Food Science. 2019;**84**:2015-2023

[37] Malav OP, Talukder S, Gokulakrishnan P, Chand S. Meat analogue: A review. Critical Reviews in Food Science and Nutrition. 2015;**55**(9):1241-1245

[38] Vital RJ, Bassinello PZ, Cruz QA, Carvalho RN, Paiva JCM, Colombo AO. Production, quality, and acceptance of tempeh and white bean tempeh burgers. Food. 2018;**7**(136):1-9

[39] Lin S, Huff HE, Hsieh F. Extrusion process parameters, sensory characteristics, and structural properties of a high moisture soy protein meat analog. J Food Sci. 2002;**67**:1066-1072

[40] Zawawi N, Gangadharan P, Ahma Zaini R, Samsudin MG, Karim R, Maznah I. Nutritional values and cooking quality of defatted kenaf seeds yellow (DKSY) noodles. International Food Research Journal. 2014;**21**(2):603-608

Chapter 5

The Possibility of Obtaining Buckwheat Beverages Fermented with Lactic Acid Bacteria and Bifidobacteria

Ewa Kowalska and Małgorzata Ziarno

Abstract

In this study, we aimed to examine the effect of four different industrial starter cultures containing lactic acid bacteria and bifidobacteria on the selected characteristics of beverages prepared from buckwheat and stored at 4°C for 28 days. We estimated the pH of the beverages during fermentation and storage under refrigerated conditions. We also determined the number of lactic acid bacteria and bifidobacteria and performed a chromatographic analysis of the carbohydrates. According to the results, the tested starter cultures effectively fermented the buckwheat beverage. The viable cell count of the starter microflora was sufficient to demonstrate the health-promoting properties of buckwheat. The pH of beverages was stable during the refrigerated storage. However, the carbohydrate content of the stored beverages changed, which indicates a constant biochemical activity of the microflora.

Keywords: buckwheat, health, lactic acid bacteria, lactic acid fermentation, bifidobacteria, probiotics

1. Introduction

In recent years, the eating habits of people have changed dramatically due to various reasons. One such reason is consumer awareness of the impact of food on human health. Products that have a natural composition, that are unprocessed, and are nongenetically modified are preferred the most by the consumers. Another important factor, which determines people's eating habits, is food allergies and intolerances, which eliminate the possibility of consumption of a particular food product. Food allergies and metabolic disorders have led to an increased demand for allergen-free food products that meet the daily requirements for protein and other nutrients. For example, in the case of gluten intolerance, it is impossible to eat food products containing gluten. For such individuals, an alternative food product is, among others, buckwheat, which, as a gluten-free pseudocereal, can be used as groats, flour in baking bread or cakes.

Buckwheat has a rich composition and high nutritional value and can be an ideal base for products that are enriched with lactic acid bacteria (LAB), including probiotics. They are defined as a functional food because when they are administered in adequate amounts, they confer specific health benefits to the consumer. Consuming

 IntechOpen

functional foods helps to reduce the risk of developing diseases of affluence, such as diabetes, obesity, or cancer. Buckwheat beverage enriched with LAB and bifidobacterial is one such functional food. Its unique taste and nutritional value might be utilized to develop a new product dedicated to people with disorders of the digestive system, as well as for people who want to stay healthy.

Fermented plant-based products represent a better way to substitute dairy products that cannot be consumed by people with food allergies or intolerance. The plant-based products gain a pro-health value after the process of fermentation and at the same time, they require minimal processing. Furthermore, the probiotic LAB have a positive effect on human health by regulating the functions of the intestinal microbiota. They keep the digestive system healthy and increase immunity. They have anticarcinogenic and antiallergenic effects [1]. Food intolerances are not related to the immune system; they are caused by sensitivity to certain food ingredients, e.g. gluten [2]. At present, approximately 20% of the population is affected due to food intolerance [3]. So far, the detailed mechanism of food intolerance is not known, but it may be related to the neuroendocrine system of the digestive system [4]. In the case of treatment available for gluten intolerance, elimination of gluten from the diet is recommended. Any amount of gluten might be harmful to individuals who are gluten-intolerant. According to the literature, more than 50–100 mg of gluten per day can prove to be harmful to such individuals [5].

2. Plant-based beverages as an alternative for dairy-based probiotic beverages

Buckwheat is a dicotyledonous plant and is referred to as a pseudocereal. It is classified as a secondary plant. It has a tap root system, which is 1 meter long, and has a straight stem, 60–90 cm high, and brown in color; it bears pink or white flowers. Different products are made from different parts of the plant. The grains are used to produce buckwheat flour and buckwheat, while straw, after threshing the seeds, is added to various types of fodder. During the flowering season, buckwheat provides nectar to the bees [6, 7]. Buckwheat kernels contain gluten-free protein and have well-balanced amino acid profile. The flour is a rich source of minerals such as copper, zinc, manganese, potassium, magnesium, phosphorus, and potassium. It is also rich in polyphenols such as rutin, orientin, vitexin, quercetin, isovitoxin, and isoorientin. Among the aforementioned polyphenols, rutin shows the strongest anti-inflammatory, anticancer, and protective effect. In terms of flavonoid content, tartar buckwheat seeds contain approximately 40 mg/g, whereas common buckwheat seeds contain 10 mg/g [8–10]. A previous study [11] reported that sucrose is the predominant sugar in buckwheat, whereas xylose, glucose, arabinose, and melibiose are present in much smaller quantities. According to a previous study [12], sucrose accumulates in large quantities when the dry matter content is increased. It mainly occurs in the central part of the ovule and the seed coat. Buckwheat also contains *R*-tocopherol, which shows vitamin E activity [13]. In addition, the ethanolic extract of buckwheat contains four catechins: epicatechin, catechin 7-O-β-D-glucopyranoside, (−)-epicatechin 3-O-p-hydroxybenzoate, and (−)-epicatechin-3-O-(3,4-di-O) gallate-methyl [13]. It should be noted that the content of individual components in the plant may change depending on the environmental factors such as temperature, UV radiation, and damage caused by pests. Genetic factors are also of great importance, and the influence of the height of cultivation to sea level has been recently demonstrated [14].

The word "probiotic" was borrowed from Greek, wherein "probios" means "for life." Probiotics are mainly bacterial strains from the genera *Lactobacillus* and *Bifidobacterium*. However, before a strain is considered a probiotic, clinical trials must be conducted to prove its health-promoting properties [15, 16]. There should be mutual benefit between the human body and the probiotic bacteria (on the basis of symbiosis). The intestines are one of the most important organs in maintaining the body's normal immunity. About 70% of the entire population of immune cells is associated with intestinal mucosa [1]. Literature shows that probiotics regulate the functioning of the bacterial microflora in the intestines through certain mechanisms [17]; for example, they compete with the pathogenic bacteria for the same receptors and nutrients; they produce lactic acid and acetic acid, which lower the pH of the environment and inhibit the colonization of pathogenic microorganisms; they produce mucus; and finally, they synthesize B vitamins.

Growing consumer needs have increased the demand for functional food, which means that the food industry introduces more and more interesting and a variety of products. Currently, Europe, Japan, and the United States are the largest markets for functional products [18]. Functional foods must contain one or more compounds that trigger specific changes in the body. In particular, they should help to reduce the risk of civilization diseases, which are the greatest threat to society; for example, cancer, diabetes, heart disease, osteoporosis, neurodegenerative diseases, and hypertension [19]. It is noteworthy that functional foods help to optimize the physiological functions of the body so that it is possible to initiate repair processes and maintain health. It cannot be treated as a drug in specific disease entities, but only as a support in therapy [20]. Compounds that can be used in functional foods are polyphenols, sterols, carotenoids, probiotics, and prebiotics [21].

There are different categories of functional foods. The simplest ones are unprocessed conventional foods, for example, tomatoes, kale, raspberries, and broccoli. These foods contain a high content of ellagic acid and lycopene. is the next category is modified foods—this category contains foods that are modified by enrichment with specific ingredients. For example, orange juice with added calcium to support bone health, bread supplemented with folic acid, which is especially dedicated to pregnant women, and margarine enriched with plant stanols. The third category of functional food is a medical food, which is used in specific disease cases and can only be administered under the supervision of a doctor. These foods include supplements for phenylketonuria and diabetes and kidney and liver disease. The latter type is special-purpose food, which includes infant formulas, gluten-free foods, lactose-free foods, and foods used in a slimming diet. Therefore, it may be one of the food products that provides the necessary nutrients. In the case of some categories of food, for example gluten-free food, some components of the material are removed to avoid the aggravation of the disease [22].

Fermented foods are grouped as functional foods. Since the beginning of human civilization, fermented foods formed the basis of food, and although people were not aware of it back then, they had a positive effect on their health [23]. Fermented foods can be obtained by the spontaneous or controlled growth of microorganisms and the enzymatic conversion of their main components. Currently, fermented foods can be produced very fast, which allows for the production of thousands of various products [24]. The fermentation process of some food products gives them new health properties and features that were not present in the starting material. Furthermore, recent clinical trials have shown an existing relationship between the consumption of fermented milk products and maintaining a healthy body weight [25]. Other studies have shown that regular consumption of fermented foods such as yogurt reduces the risk of heart disease and type 2 diabetes [26, 27].

3. Buckwheat beverages fermented with industrial probiotic cultures

In this study, we aimed to investigate the effect of four different bacterial cultures containing LAB and bifidobacteria on the selected features of buckwheat beverage. With regard to this, we performed fermentation of the selected cultures with buckwheat beverages and evaluated the parameters.

Fermented plant beverages are very popular in Asia and Africa, for example, boza, togwa, mahewu, makgeolli, or hardalie. The most popular plant-based fermented beverage in Poland and throughout Eastern Europe is kvass. It is a product of milk-alcohol fermentation of wholemeal bread with the addition of yeast, water, and a small amount of sugar. The microorganisms present in kvass are *Lactobacillus casei*, *Leuconostoc mesenteroides*, and *Saccharomyces cerevisiae* [28].

In recent years, many studies have reported the properties of plant-based fermented beverages. The most important feature of this type of product is the ability of LAB to carry out effective fermentation, and the pH value of the resulting product is an important parameter, which indicates the effectiveness of the fermentation process. In this study, this parameter was checked both during the fermentation process and after its completion (28 days).

Kowalska [29] used four yogurt starter cultures to ferment the buckwheat beverage: YO-MIX 207, YO-MIX 205, ABY-3, and VEGE 033. The microbial composition of the starters was as follows:

a. ABY-3 (Chr. Hansen, Denmark)—Streptococcus thermophilus, Lactobacillus delbrueckii subsp. bulgaricus, Lactobacillus acidophilus La-5, Bifidobacterium animalis subsp. lactis BB-12,

b. YO-MIX 207 (DuPont Danisco, Denmark)—*S. thermophilus*, L. delbrueckii subsp. bulgaricus, L. acidophilus, Bifidobacterium lactis,

c. YO-MIX 205 LYO (DuPont Danisco, Denmark)—*S. thermophilus*, L. delbrueckii subsp. bulgaricus, L. acidophilus, B. lactis,

d. VEGE 033 LYO (DuPont Danisco, Denmark)—*S. thermophilus*, L. delbrueckii subsp. bulgaricus, L. acidophilus NCFM, B. lactis HN019.

Buckwheat beverage was prepared with 200 g of boiled buckwheat and blended with 3000 mL of drinking water. Prior to the process of sterilization, the beverage was strained through a fine sieve to get rid of the groats. The strained beverage was sterilized at 121°C for 15 min [30]. Based on the recipe of the buckwheat beverage, which was obtained by mixing the buckwheat in water in the proportion 1:15, the nutritional value of 100 g of buckwheat beverage was calculated [29]:

- Fat—0.16 g (including 0.04 g of saturated acids)
- Carbohydrates—4.69 g (including 0.16 g of sugars)
- Proteins—0.75 g.

The average water content of buckwheat beverage was 87.9% [30].

Kowalska [29] reported that the initial pH of buckwheat (beverage before fermentation at 37°C for 5 h) was on an average 6.550 for the samples intended for fermentation with YO-MIX 207, YO-MIX 205, and ABY-3 cultures, and 6.400 for the samples intended for fermentation with VEGE 033 culture (**Table 1**). The most effective fermentation process was observed in the case of beverage fermented with YO-MIX 207 culture, followed by the beverage fermented with YO-MIX 205. Within 1–2 h of fermentation, both beverages reached an average pH value of 4.8, which was statistically significantly from that of before fermentation (**Table 1**). ABY3 and VEGE 033 cultures were less efficient in terms of acidification, in which case, the pH value did not increase until 3–4 h of the fermentation process. After fermentation for 5 h, all of the beverages reached a pH of 4.5–4.9, which means that all the bacteria carried out the fermentation process efficiently [29]. A previous study [31] also reported similar results for soybean beverage fermented with *S. thermophilus*. However, a previous study [32] conducted on barley malt fermented with *Lactobacillus plantarum* (NCIMB 8826) and *L. acidophilus* (NCIMB 8821) recorded a pH value of approximately 4.0. This difference in pH value might be because of the specificity of plant matrices, as well as the use of various bacterial cultures for fermentation (**Table 2**).

Kowalska [29] also measured the pH of buckwheat beverage during 28 days of refrigerated storage. During refrigerated storage, the most stable pH value was recorded for buckwheat beverage fermented with VEGE 033, ABY-3, and YO-MIX 205 cultures. However, the beverage fermented with YO-MIX 207 culture showed variation in pH value during refrigerated storage.

Table 1 shows the pH value of buckwheat beverage before and after fermentation with cultures tested by Kowalska [29]. Similar results were obtained by Ziarno et al. [33]. They reported the change in pH value of bean beverage (initial pH of 6.58) after fermentation, which was 4.47 and 4.45 when fermented with YO-MIX 205 and ABY-3 cultures, respectively. At 6°C, the pH value of beverages fermented with YO-MIX 205 and ABY-3 cultures respectively decreased to 4.40 and 4.39 on day 7, 4.34 and 4.29 on day 21, and 4.33 and 4.27 on day 28 [33]. This shows that LAB continued the process of fermentation during the entire storage period, which was not observed in the research conducted by Kowalska [29].

Bacterial cell count is a very important parameter in determining the quality of the product and its health properties [34]. Manufacturers frequently check this parameter in fermented beverages. The minimum acceptable number of live LAB cells that should be present in fermented beverages is 7 log(CFU/mL) and at least 6 log(CFU/mL) for strains with probiotic properties, including probiotics of the genus *Bifidobacterium* [35].

Kowalska [29] found that the changes in the number of live LAB and bifidobacteria in beverages fermented with the YO-MIX 205 and YO-MIX 207 cultures were

Fermentation time [h]	Buckwheat beverages fermented by:			
	YO-MIX 207	YO-MIX 205	ABY-3	VEGE 033
0	6.550 ± 0.212^{a}	6.550 ± 0.212^{a}	6.550 ± 0.212^{a}	6.400 ± 0.000^{a}
1	5.185 ± 0.481^{b}	5.020 ± 0.389^{b}	5.610 ± 0.721^{ab}	5.770 ± 0.000^{ab}
2	4.840 ± 0.226^{b}	4.805 ± 0.163^{b}	5.085 ± 0.262^{b}	5.170 ± 0.000^{b}
3	4.730 ± 0.127^{b}	4.675 ± 0.163^{b}	4.860 ± 0.085^{b}	4.910 ± 0.000^{b}
4	4.640 ± 0.057^{b}	4.600 ± 0.212^{b}	4.825 ± 0.106^{b}	4.880 ± 0.000^{b}
5	4.590 ± 0.127^{b}	4.595 ± 0.276^{b}	4.790 ± 0.156^{b}	4.950 ± 0.000^{b}

Note: ^{a,b}—values in columns with the same letter do not differ statistically significantly for $\alpha = 0.05$.

Table 1.
pH values of buckwheat beverage during the fermentation process (mean ± standard deviation) (based on [29]).

Storage time [day]	Buckwheat beverage fermented by:			
	YO-MIX 207	YO-MIX 207	YO-MIX 207	YO-MIX 207
0	4.590 ± 0.127[b]	4.595 ± 0.276[a]	4.790 ± 0.156[a]	4.950 ± 0.000[a]
7	4.750 ± 0.071[ab]	4.750 ± 0.071[a]	4.850 ± 0.071[a]	4.900 ± 0.000[a]
21	4.875 ± 0.035[ab]	4.850 ± 0.071[a]	4.850 ± 0.071[a]	5.000 ± 0.000[a]
28	4.920 ± 0.028[a]	4.935 ± 0.049[a]	4.925 ± 0.035[a]	5.000 ± 0.000[a]

Note: [a,b]—values in columns with the same letter do not differ statistically significantly for $\alpha = 0.05$.

Table 2.
pH values of buckwheat beverage fermented with different starter cultures (mean values and standard deviations) (based on [29]).

very similar. Interestingly, after fermentation, there was a slight reduction in the number of viable bacterial cells compared to the state before fermentation. In addition, during the refrigerated storage of the fermented beverage, there were fluctuations in the number of LAB cells, both lactobacilli and lactic streptococci, as well as bifidobacteria. The number of viable cells of lactobacilli, lactic streptococci, and bifidobacteria on day 28 was over 7 log(CFU/mL), which indicated the potential health-promoting properties of the tested beverages fermented with the YO-MIX 207 and YO-MIX 205 cultures.

The smallest variation in the population of lactobacilli, lactic streptococci, and bifidobacteria was recorded for beverages fermented with ABY-3 culture (**Table 3**) [29]. Contrary to buckwheat beverages fermented with the YO-MIX 207 (**Table 4**) and YO-MIX 205 (**Table 5**), there were no such significant changes in the number of bacterial cells. After fermentation, the number of bifidobacterial cells decreased the most. After 7 days of refrigerated storage (4°C), there was a slight change in the number of lactobacilli, lactic streptococci, and bifidobacteria. After 28 days of storage, the average bacterial cell count was 8.0 log(CFU/mL) for lactobacilli, 7.8 log(CFU/mL) for lactic streptococci, and 8.0 log(CFU/mL) for bifidobacteria. The number of viable cells of lactobacilli, lactic streptococci, and bifidobacteria on day 28 was over 7 log(CFU/mL), which indicated the potentially health-promoting properties of the tested buckwheat beverages fermented with the ABY-3 culture [29].

According to Kowalska [29], in the case of buckwheat beverage fermented with VEGE 033 (**Table 6**), the greatest proportion in the population of bacterial cells prior to fermentation were lactic streptococci [29]. In the beverages fermented with the VEGE 033 culture, the lower number of bifidobacterial cells was found (during the entire period of cooling storage) compared to the buckwheat beverage fermented with ABY-3 culture. On the 7th day of storage of the samples of buckwheat beverages fermented with the VEGE 033 culture, the number of streptococcal cells was on average 8.2 log(CFU/mL). The number of viable lactobacilli, lactic streptococci, and bifidobacteria cells in the beverage fermented with VEGE 033 culture on day 28 was over 7 log(CFU/mL) [29].

A previous study conducted on rice beverage reported low counts of bacterial cells [36]. Prior to fermentation, the number of bacterial cells in rice beverage was lower than that observed for buckwheat beverage in the research conducted by Kowalska [29] - the population of LAB was 5.0 log(CFU/mL). However, after 16-hour fermentation process, the bacterial population increased to 8.1 log(CFU/mL) and remained at this level until the end of the fermentation process [29]. However, the previous study [37] reported that after fermentation of corn or rice-based beverages, the microbial cell population was at the level of 7–8 log(CFU/mL). This number indicates that the product has probiotic properties [38].

Determination time	Number of lactobacilli [log(CFU/mL)]	Number of bifidobacteria [log(CFU/mL)]	Number of lactic streptococci [log(CFU/mL)]
Before fermentation	8.2 ± 0.2[a]	8.2 ± 0.4[a]	8.2 ± 0.4[a]
After fermentation	7.9 ± 0.3[a]	7.7 ± 0.1[b]	8.0 ± 0.3[a]
7 day of storage	8.1 ± 0.3[a]	8.2 ± 0.2[ab]	8.0 ± 0.2[a]
28 days of storage	8.0 ± 0.2[a]	8.0 ± 0.2[ab]	7.8 ± 0.1[a]

Note: [a,b]—values in columns with the same letter do not differ statistically significantly for $\alpha = 0.05$.

Table 3.
The population of live cells of lactic acid bacteria and bifidobacteria in buckwheat beverage fermented with ABY-3 culture and stored for 28 days under refrigerated condition (mean ± standard deviation) (based on [29]).

Determination time	Number of lactobacilli [log(CFU/mL)]	Number of bifidobacteria [log(CFU/mL)]	Number of lactic streptococci [log(CFU/mL)]
Before fermentation	8.7 ± 0.3[a]	8.5 ± 0.2[a]	8.4 ± 1.1[a]
After fermentation	7.8 ± 0.2[b]	7.2 ± 0.1[c]	7.9 ± 0.3[a]
7 day of storage	8.0 ± 0.3[b]	8.1 ± 0.3[ab]	8.0 ± 0.4[a]
28 days of storage	7.8 ± 0.0[b]	7.7 ± 0.1[b]	7.7 ± 0.3[a]

Note: [a–c]—values in columns with the same letter do not differ statistically significantly for $\alpha = 0.05$.

Table 4.
The population of live cells of lactic acid bacteria and bifidobacteria in buckwheat beverage fermented with YO-MIX 207 culture and stored for 28 days under refrigerated condition (mean ± standard deviation) (based on [29]).

Determination time	Number of lactobacilli [log(CFU/mL)]	Number of bifidobacteria [log(CFU/mL)]	Number of lactic streptococci [log(CFU/mL)]
Before fermentation	7.9 ± 0.8[a]	7.8 ± 0.7[a]	8.4 ± 0.8[a]
After fermentation	7.6 ± 0.2[a]	7.0 ± 0.2[a]	7.8 ± 0.5[a]
7 day of storage	7.9 ± 0.6[a]	7.6 ± 0.7[a]	8.1 ± 0.5[a]
28 days of storage	7.6 ± 0.1[a]	7.5 ± 0.3[a]	7.8 ± 0.2[a]

Note: [a]—values in columns with the same letter do not differ statistically significantly for $\alpha = 0.05$.

Table 5.
The population of live cells of lactic acid bacteria and bifidobacteria in buckwheat beverage fermented with YO-MIX 205 culture and stored for 28 days under refrigerated conditions (mean ± standard deviation) (based on [29]).

However, another group of researchers [39] used different strains of LAB for fermentation of soy milk, including *L. delbrueckii* subsp. bulgaricus and *L. acidophilus*, which were also used in this study. The cell population of all cultures was 8 log(CFU/mL), which is similar to the results of this study with buckwheat. In each bacterial culture, *L. delbrueckii* subsp. bulgaricus and *L. acidophilus* were present, but their strain was different.

Kowalska [29] found that in all plant-based products, there were similarities in the population of LAB, despite the diversity of the *Lactobacillus* strains used. The

Determination time	Number of lactobacilli [log(CFU/mL)]	Number of bifidobacteria [log(CFU/mL)]	Number of lactic streptococci [log(CFU/mL)]
Before fermentation	8.7 ± 0.0[a]	7.1 ± 0.1[b]	9.0 ± 0.1[a]
After fermentation	7.1 ± 0.1[d]	7.3 ± 0.0[b]	7.9 ± 0.0[c]
7 day of storage	8.1 ± 0.1[b]	8.2 ± 0.2[a]	8.2 ± 0.1[b]
28 days of storage	7.7 ± 0.0[c]	7.4 ± 0.1[b]	7.5 ± 0.0[d]

Note: [a–d]—values in columns with the same letter do not differ statistically significantly for α = 0.05.

Table 6.
The population of live cells of lactic acid bacteria and bifidobacteria in buckwheat beverage fermented with VEGE 033 culture and stored for 28 days under refrigerated condition (mean ± standard deviation) (based on [29]).

good growth of LAB in plant-based beverages can be explained by the high amounts of mono and disaccharides in the plant media.

A previous study performed fermentation of bean beverages with ABY-3 culture [33]. Prior to fermentation, the number of viable lactobacilli was 7.7 log(CFU/mL), which gradually decreased during the cold storage. On days 7 and 28 of storage, the population of lactobacilli was 7.5 log(CFU/mL) and 6.9 log(CFU/mL), respectively. According to a previous study [30], the observed lower bacterial cells after the cold storage period may result from antimicrobial compounds produced by bacteria, e.g. hydrogen peroxide, bacteriocins, or organic acids. In contrast, in the research conducted by Kowalska [29], the number of viable lactobacilli in the buckwheat beverage fermented with ABY-3 culture was slightly higher. Prior to fermentation, on days 7 and 28 of storage, the number of viable lactobacilli was 8.2 log(CFU/mL) and 8.0 log(CFU/mL), respectively. The better growth on buckwheat substrate might be due to higher sugar content and availability in plant media.

Kowalska [29] verified the content of carbohydrates using high-performance liquid chromatography. The results showed the presence of 7 carbohydrates: xylose, melibiose, fructose, arabinose, glucose, sucrose, and maltose. The initial (before fermentation) content of carbohydrate in the fermented buckwheat beverage was 4.598 g in 100 g of the product. The chromatographic analysis includes only a few selected carbohydrates, whereas the calculated value of carbohydrate content takes into account all such compounds, including starch. Therefore, it can be concluded that as a result of the cooking and sterilization of buckwheat beverage in an aqueous solution, some complex carbohydrates or polysaccharides might be released, which were determined by chromatography [29].

Immediately after the end of fermentation of buckwheat beverages, the highest total carbohydrate content was found in the beverage fermented with the ABY-3 culture (**Table 7**), whereas the lowest was found in the beverage fermented with the YO-MIX 207 culture (**Table 8**). It should be noted that both the ABY-3 culture and the YO-MIX 207 culture had a rich microbiological composition, which not only included LAB but also included bifidobacteria of different strains [29].

In the case of beverage fermented with YO-MIX 205 culture (**Table 9**), we obtained statistically significant differences in terms of carbohydrate content before and after fermentation and during cold storage.

Contrary to the buckwheat beverages fermented with the YO-MIX 205 and YO-MIX 207 cultures, the beverage fermented with VEGE 033 culture (**Table 10**) contained a low amount of xylose after fermentation. In this case, the xylose content decreased slightly. As in the beverages fermented with the

Carbohydrates [g/100 g beverage]	Before fermentation	After fermentation	After 7 days of storage	After 28 days of storage
Xylose	0.000[e]	0.129[e]	0.065[f]	0.193[b]
Fructose	0.096[d]	0.322[b]	0.132[e]	0.000[e]
Arabinose	0.000[e]	0.241[d]	0.294[c]	0.000[e]
Glucose	2.958[a]	0.280[c]	0.251[d]	0.152[c]
Melibiose	0.000[e]	0.000[f]	0.318[b]	0.153[c]
Sucrose	1.544[b]	2.300[a]	1.591[a]	0.698[a]
Maltose	0.218[c]	0.000[f]	0.000[g]	0.000[e]
All	4.598	3.273	2.650	1.196

Note: [a–e]—values in columns with the same letter do not differ statistically significantly for α = 0.05.

Table 7.
Content of carbohydrates in buckwheat beverages fermented with ABY-3 culture (based on [29]).

Carbohydrates [g/100 g beverage]	Before fermentation	After fermentation	After 7 days of storage	After 28 days of storage
Xylose	0.000[f]	0.000[f]	0.000[e]	0.143[c]
Fructose	0.096[d]	0.115[c]	0.076[d]	0.164[b]
Arabinose	0.000[e]	0.069[d]	0.086[c]	0.000[g]
Glucose	2.958[a]	0.204[b]	0.186[b]	0.102[d]
Melibiose	0.000[e]	0.000[e]	0.000[f]	0.087[e]
Sucrose	1.544[b]	1.436[a]	1.388[a]	0.751[a]
Maltose	0.218[c]	0.000[f]	0.000[f]	0.000[f]
All	4.598	1.824	1.736	1.247

Note: [a–g]—values in columns with the same letter do not differ statistically significantly for α = 0.05.

Table 8.
Content of carbohydrates in buckwheat beverages fermented with YO-MIX 207 culture (based on [29]).

YO-MIX 205 and YO-MIX 207 cultures, the content of sucrose, glucose, and maltose also decreased, and the content of arabinose increased. The chromatographic analysis also did not detect the presence of melibiose. Statistical analysis showed significant differences in the results of carbohydrate content during cold storage of the samples.

Our results show differences in the fermentation abilities of the tested starter cultures, resulting from different biochemical activities (mainly saccharolytic and fermentation) of the strains present in the tested cultures [29].

It can be assumed that the changes in the content of carbohydrates during refrigerated storage were due to the changes taking place in the analyzed samples; for example, the biochemical activity of LAB and bifidobacteria, as well as enzymatic changes [29]. Due to the lack of information, it is difficult to compare the results of this study with that of others.

A previous study [40] reported contradictory results with respect to sugar content in the cooked buckwheat wort. According to the result of the aforementioned study, glucose was present in the highest quantities. However, in this study, sucrose was found to be the highest after fermentation and after the storage period, which was most likely the result of starch decomposition.

Carbohydrates [g/100 g beverage]	Before fermentation	After fermentation	After 7 days of storage	After 28 days of storage
Xylose	0.000^{e}	0.000^{e}	0.042^{e}	0.233^{c}
Fructose	0.096^{d}	0.099^{d}	0.093^{d}	0.244^{b}
Arabinose	0.000^{e}	0.152^{c}	0.873^{b}	0.000^{f}
Glucose	2.958^{a}	0.000^{e}	0.000^{f}	0.123^{d}
Melibiose	0.000^{e}	0.286^{b}	0.188^{c}	0.075^{e}
Sucrose	1.544^{b}	1.514^{a}	1.763^{a}	0.595^{a}
Maltose	0.218^{c}	0.000^{e}	0.000^{f}	0.000^{f}
All	4.598	2.051	2.959	1.270

Note: $^{a-f}$—values in columns with the same letter do not differ statistically significantly for $\alpha = 0.05$.

Table 9.
Content of carbohydrates in buckwheat beverages fermented with YO-MIX 205 culture (based on [29]).

Carbohydrates [g/100 g beverage]	Before fermentation	After fermentation	After 7 days of storage	After 28 days of storage
Xylose	0.000^{e}	0.080^{e}	0.625^{c}	0.705^{a}
Fructose	0.096^{d}	0.094^{d}	0.000^{e}	0.000^{e}
Arabinose	0.000^{e}	0.741^{b}	1.299^{b}	0.264^{c}
Glucose	2.958^{a}	0.237^{c}	0.328^{d}	0.106^{d}
Melibiose	0.000^{e}	0.000^{f}	0.000^{e}	0.000^{e}
Sucrose	1.544^{b}	1.237^{a}	1.598^{a}	0.338^{b}
Maltose	0.218^{c}	0.000^{f}	0.000^{e}	0.000^{e}
All	4.598	2.389	3.851	1.413

Note: $^{a-f}$—values in columns with the same letter do not differ statistically significantly for $\alpha = 0.05$.

Table 10.
Content of carbohydrates in buckwheat beverages fermented by VEGE 033 culture (based on [29]).

A previous study [41] reported that sucrose was the predominant carbohydrate, whereas xylose, glucose, arabinose, and melibiose were present in much smaller quantities. Another study [42] reported that with an increasing amount of water and lengthening heating time, the content of glucose increases.

According to the literature [43], fermentation of buckwheat beverages with the use of *Propionibacterium freudenreichii* subsp. *shermanii* resulted in a significant increase in the content of fructose, glucose, and galactose. In addition, there was a significant increase in sucrose content.

4. Conclusion

The results of this study indicate a high potential of fermented buckwheat beverage as a probiotic product with pro-health properties. The demand for gluten-free cereal beverages is growing among people suffering from celiac disease and food intolerance. Good bacterial survival during the storage period allows achieving a therapeutic effect similar to that caused by consuming fermented milk products, such as kefir, buttermilk, or yoghurt. In addition, an additional advantage of the product is the lack of allergenic milk proteins. More and more people are experiencing side effects after drinking milk and other dairy products such as gas, indigestion, and diarrhea, which are causing them to be excluded from their diet. In such a case, dietary supplements containing probiotic strains are often used to supplement the intestinal microflora and increase the body's immunity. Fermented buckwheat beverages can replace these types of supplements and provide other essential nutrients for the body. The product is dedicated not only to people suffering from disorders of the digestive system but also to healthy people who care about a balanced diet and want to have a healthy lifestyle. In addition to LAB and bifidobacteria, the base of the buckwheat beverage is important, as it is also a medium necessary for the growth of the bacterial population used for fermentation. Our results show that buckwheat can be successfully fermented by LAB and bifidobacteria. Its proven health properties mean that the beverage can be used to prevent civilization diseases such as diabetes, obesity, or cancer.

Acknowledgements

This work was supported by a grant from Warsaw University of Life Sciences - WULS-SGGW.

Conflict of interest

Authors have declared that they do not have any conflict of interest in publishing this research.

Author details

Ewa Kowalska[1*] and Małgorzata Ziarno[2]

1 Institute of Horticultural Sciences, Warsaw University of Life Sciences - SGGW (WULS-SGGW), Warsaw, Poland

2 Division of Milk Technology, Department of Food Technology and Assessment, Institute of Food Science, Warsaw University of Life Sciences - SGGW (WULS-SGGW), Warsaw, Poland

*Address all correspondence to: kowalska.ewa.95@wp.pl

References

[1] Nowak A., Slizewska K., Libudzisz Z.: Probiotyki-historia i mechanizmy dzialania. Żywność Nauka Technologia Jakość. 2010; 17(4), 5-19 (in Polish, Abstract in English)

[2] Turnbull JL, Adams HN, Gorard DA. The diagnosis and management of food allergy and food intolerances. Alimentary Pharmacology and Therapeutics. 2015;**41**(1):3-25

[3] Zopf Y, Baenkler HW, Silbermann A, Hahn EG, Raithel M. The differential diagnosis of food intolerance. Deutsches Ärzteblatt International. 2009;**106**:359-369

[4] Lomer MCE. The aetiology, diagnosis, mechanisms and clinical evidence for food intolerance. Alimentary Pharmacology and Therapeutics. 2015;**41**(3):262-275

[5] Hischenhuber C, Crevel R, Jarry B, Maki M, Moneret-Vautrin DA, Romano A, et al. Review article: Safe amounts of gluten for patients with wheat allergy or coeliac disease. Alimentary Pharmacology and Therapeutics. 2006;**23**:559-575

[6] Zarzecka K., Marek G., Iwona M.: Nutritional and pro-health value of buckwheat. Problemy Higieny i Epidemiologii. 2015; 96(2), 410-413 (in Polish, Abstract in English)

[7] Grochowicz J., Dominik P., Fabisiak A. The possibilities of using natural foods as a result of the global trend in food demand health prevention. Zeszyty Naukowe Uczelni Vistula. 2017; 54.3. Turystyka III, 223-240 (in Polish, Abstract in English)

[8] Kawakami A, Inbe T, Kayahara H, Horii A. Preparation of enzymatic hydrolysates of buckwheat globulin and their angiotensin I converting enzyme inhibitory activities. Current Advances in Buckwheat Research. 1995;**1**:927-934

[9] Christa K, Soral-Smietana M. Buckwheat grains and buckwheat products nutritional and prophylactic value of their components- a review. Czech Journal of Food Sciences. 2008;**26**:153-162

[10] Ikeda S, Tomura K, Yamashita Y, Kreft I. Minerals in buckwheat flour subjected to enzymatic digestion. Fagopyrum. 2001;**18**:45-48

[11] Campbell CG. Buckwheat: *Fagopyrum esculentum* Moench. Kanada: International Plant Genetic Resources Institute; 1997

[12] Duffus CM, Binnie J. Sucrose relationships during endosperm and embryo development in wheat. Plant Physiology and Biochemistry. 1990;**28**(2):161-165

[13] Kalinova J, Triska J, Vrchotova N. Distribution of vitamin E, squalene, epicatechin and rutin in common buckwheat plants (Fagopyrum esculentum Moench). Journal of Agricultural and Food Chemistry. 2006;**54**:5330-5335

[14] Zhang ZL, Zhou ML, Tang Y, Li FL, Tang YX, Shao JR, et al. Bioactive compounds in functional buckwheat food. Food Research International. 2012;**49**(1):389-395

[15] Schaafsama G.: State-of-the-art concerning probiotic strains in milk products. International Dairy Federation, Nutrition Newsletter. 1996; 5, 23-24 83

[16] Dominguez-Bello MG, Blaser MJ. Do you have a probiotic in your future? Microbes an Infection. 2008;**10**:1072-1076

[17] Egert M, de Graaf A, Smidt H, de Vos W, Venema K. Beyond diversity: functional microbiomics of the human colon. Trends in Microbiology. 2006;**14**:86-91

[18] Blandon J., Cranfield J., Henson S.: Functional Food and Natural Health Product Issues: The Canadian and International Context. International Food Economy Research Group Department of Food, Agricultural and Resource Economics, University of Guelph, Kanada. 2007

[19] Arihara K., Nakashima Y., Ishikawa S., Itoh M.: Antihypertensive activities generated from porcine skeletal muscle proteins by lactic acid bacteria. In: Abstracts of 50th International Congress of Meat Science and Technology; Aug 8-13 2004, Helsinki, Finlandis, Elsevier

[20] Sanders ME. Overview of functional foods: emphasis on probiotic bacteria. International Dairy Journal. 1998;**8**:341-347

[21] Granato D, Castro IA, Masson ML, Ribeiro JCB. Sensory evaluation and physicochemical optimization of soy-based desserts using response surface methodology. Food Chemistry. 2010;**121**:899-906

[22] ADA: Position of the American Dietetic Association: functional foods. Journal of the American Dietetic Association. 2009; 109, 735-46

[23] Hutkins RW. Microbiology and Technology of Fermented Foods. WileyBlackwell. 2008

[24] Marco ML, Heeney D, Binda S, Cifelli CJ, Cotter PD, Foligné B, et al. Health benefits of fermented foods: microbiota and beyond. Current Opinion in Biotechnology. 2017;**44**:94-102

[25] Mozaffarian D. Changes in diet and lifestyle and long-term weight gain in women and men. The New England Journal of Medicine. 2011;**364**:2392-2404

[26] Chen M, Sun Q, Giovannucci E, Mozaffarian D, Manson JE, Willett WC, et al. Dairy consumption and risk of type 2 diabetes: 3 cohorts of US adults and an updated metaanalysis. BMC Medicine. 2014;**12**(1):215

[27] Tapsell LC. Fermented dairy food and CVD risk. British Journal of Nutrition. 2015;**113**:131-135

[28] Dziugan P., Dziedziczak K., Ambroziak W.: Błonnik w pieczywie. Cukiernictwo i Piekarstwo. 2006; 10 (05), 60-62 (in Polish, Abstract in English)

[29] Kowalska E. The influence of lactic acid bacteria and bifidobacteria on selected characteristics of fermented buckwheat beverages. 2019. [thesis] (in Polish, Abstract in English)

[30] Hassan AA, Aly MM, El-Hadidie ST. Production of cereal-based probiotic beverages. World Applied Sciences Journal. 2012;**19**(10):1367-1380

[31] Champagne CP, Green-Johnson J, Raymond Y, Barrette J, Buckley N. Selection of probiotic bacteria for the fermentation of a soy beverage in combination with Streptococcus thermophilus. Food Research International. 2009;**42**:612-621

[32] Rathore S, Salmerón I, Pandiella SS. Production of potentially probiotic beverages using single and mixed cereal substrates fermented with lactic acid bacteria cultures. Food Microbiology. 2012;**30**(1):239-244

[33] Ziarno M, Zaręba D, Maciejak M, Veber AL. The impact of dairy starter cultures on selected qualitative

properties of functional fermented beverage prepared from germinated White Kidney Beans. Journal of Food and Nutrition Research. 2019;**2**:167-176 ISSN: 1338-4260

[34] Zareba D, Ziarno M, Ścibisz I, Gawron J. The importance of volatile compound profile in the assessment of fermentation conducted by Lactobacillus casei DN-114001. International Dairy Journal. 2014;**35**:11-14

[35] Mituniewicz-Małek A, Ziarno M, Dmytrów I, Balejko J. Effect of the addition of Bifidobacterium monocultures on the physical, chemical and sensory characteristics of fermented goat milk. Journal of Dairy Science. 2017;**100**:6972-6979

[36] Ramos CL, de Almeida EG, Freire AL, Schwan RF. Diversity of bacteria and yeast in the naturally fermented cotton seed and rice beverage produced by Brazilian Amerindians. Food Microbiology. 2011;**28**(7):1380-1386

[37] Němečková I, Dragounova H, Pechačová M, Rysova J, Roubal P. Fermentation of vegetable substrates by lactic acid bacteria as a basis of functional foods. Czech Journal of Food Sciences. 2012;**29**:42-48

[38] FAO/WHO: Codex Alimentarius Commision. Annex Proposed Draft Standard for Fermented Milks. 1997

[39] Santos AD, Auler CC, Da Silva Libeck B, Schwan RF. Co-culture fermentation of peanut-soy milk for the development of a novel functional beverage. International Journal of Food Microbiology. 2014;**186**:32-41

[40] Phiarais NPB, Mauch A, Schehl DB, Zarnkow M, Gastl M, Herrmann M, et al. Processing of a top fermented beer brewed from 100% buckwheat malt with sensory and analytical characterisation. Journal of the Institute of Brewing. 2010;**116**(3):265-274

[41] Campbell C. G.: Buckwheat: Fagopyrum esculentum Moench. International Plant Genetic Resources Institute. 1997, Canada

[42] Zondag MD. Effect of microwave heat-moisture and annealing treatments on buckwheat starch characteristics. Research Paper: University of Wisconsin, Stout; 2003

[43] Wajcht M. Research on the use of *Propionibacterium* sp. in the production of fermented milk and vegetable drinks, Warsaw University of Life Sciences; 2019. [thesis] (in Polish, Abstract in English)

Chapter 6

Functional Fermented Beverage Prepared from Germinated White Kidney Beans (*Phaseolus vulgaris* L.)

Anna Veber, Dorota Zaręba and Małgorzata Ziarno

Abstract

The current demand for plant-based food indicates that the food market is providing alternatives for products that are currently commercially available. This chapter discusses the possible use of germinated bean seeds as a raw material in the production of substitutes for dairy products, including fermented ones. Beans are a valuable source of easily digestible protein, carbohydrates, minerals, and various vitamins (e.g., B vitamin group). They also contain significant amounts of fiber which affects the proper functioning of the digestive system and antioxidant compounds. The fat content is low and is estimated to be around only 1–2%. However, it is mainly (about 70%) constituted by unsaturated fatty acids, including the polyunsaturated ones such as linoleic acid or linolenic acid, which are desirable in the human diet for the prevention of cardiovascular diseases or cancer. Biological processes such as germination or fermentation may improve the nutritional value of bean seeds (by increasing the content, digestibility, and bioavailability of some nutrients and by eliminating undesirable components) and deliver live cells of prohealth bacteria (lactic acid bacteria, propionic acid bacteria, or bifidobacteria).

Keywords: bean-based beverages, white kidney beans, germination, fermentation, lactic acid bacteria, bifidobacteria

1. Introduction

Common bean (*Phaseolus vulgaris* L.) is an annual angiosperm belonging to the Fabaceae family. It originates from Central and South America, where it was cultivated as early as 7000 years ago. Due to their ability to self-pollinate, beans can produce seeds after pollination with pollen from their own flower [1]. There are about 200 species identified so far, of which the first known were green pods with dark seeds. Based on the evolutionary rate, organisms of the genus *Phaseolus* are estimated to be about six million years old, which suggests that it is a relatively young group of plants [2, 3]. Currently, most varieties of beans are cultivated for food, on all continents and in various climatic zones [1].

Bean varieties are classified into two main groups: dwarf and tic. In the case of dwarf varieties, a poorly developed stem reaches 60 cm, whereas in climbing varieties, the stem can grow up to 200–300 cm. Features such as shape, color, and size of the pods are related to the variety. There is a relationship between the shape of the seeds and the shape of the pod. Elongated and cylindrical seeds are found in round and long pods, while flattened seeds are found in flat pods. The bean fruit is an elongated pod, which varies in color, shape, and fiber content, depending on the variety.

Beans are one of the most important plants that are directly consumed in the world. Due to their nutritional and health benefits, they are used in many dishes and are also consumed by people following vegan and vegetarian diets as a valuable source of vegetable protein. In some regions, such as South and Central American and African countries, beans are a staple in the daily diet and usually consumed after soaking and cooking.

Consuming the seeds of legumes, which include beans, can result in many physiological and health benefits, including the prevention of cardiovascular disease, diabetes, and cancer. Beans are high-fiber, high-protein vegetables that contain a less amount of fats. They are valuable sources of not only easily digestible protein but also minerals and various vitamins (e.g., B vitamins). Furthermore, they contain a wide range of phytochemical and antioxidant compounds, including flavonoids, such as anthocyanins, flavonols, phenolic acids, and isoflavones, which are compounds regulating the expression of genes responsible for the processes of β-fat oxidation, lithogenesis, and hepatic gluconeogenesis. Beans are also rich in oligosaccharides, lectins, saponins, phytates, and polyphenolic compounds, the main classes of which are tannins, phenolic acids, and flavonoids. Phenolic extracts from various types of beans exhibit antioxidant properties [4]. The polyphenolic components present in beans are mainly concentrated in the seed coat and give the seeds their color. Legume seeds also have a lower glycemic index compared to other starchy foods such as cereals and potatoes. When added in the daily diet, legumes can exert many beneficial physiological effects and prevent common metabolic diseases such as diabetes, coronary artery disease, and cancer [5–7]. They are effective in lowering blood pressure, normalizing body weight and lipid metabolism, reducing insulin resistance, and thus regulating the components of the metabolic syndrome and are therefore recommended for its prevention and treatment [8].

Use of the germination of bean seeds and then the fermentation process of beverages obtained from the germinated bean seeds allow to increase the health and nutritional values of these beverages. This chapter presents various studies about technology, quality, and nutritional value of fermented bean-based beverages prepared from germinated white kidney beans (*Phaseolus vulgaris* L.).

2. Preparation of beverages from beans

Plant milk substitutes are obtained mainly by water extraction of selected plant material. The production process is of different types, depending on the raw material used (legumes, cereals, vegetables, nuts, seeds), but all the variants have a common outline. Generally, the preparation process involves the following stages: selection of the raw material, soaking and wet or dry grinding of the raw material, water extraction of the raw material, heating, separation of the solid fraction, cooling, standardization, homogenization, thermal fixation, aseptic packaging, and storage [9–12].

In some cases, additional blanching or roasting of the raw material is carried out prior to soaking and grinding. Blanching is usually done in boiling water for 1–5 minutes, for example, to inactivate trypsin and lipoxygenase inhibitors in the case of soybean beverages. Moreover, it prevents the formation of foam during the technological process. Roasting is carried out at a temperature above 100°C, in hot air, and its duration is determined by the type of the raw material and the temperature of the process. This process is used to improve the taste and aroma of the final product; however, it may reduce the protein solubility and extraction efficiency [9]. In the case of bean-based beverages, before soaking and grinding the seeds, it is advisable to carry out germination [10, 12].

Soaking and grinding (or only grinding) of the raw material are employed for further processing steps and to facilitate the release of nutrients contained in it. Water inactivates some of the inhibitors and reduces the amount of phytic acid, which increases the absorption of nutrients and their bioavailability [9–14]. In the case of beans, wet grinding is performed after thermal treatment of the seeds to induce starch thermohydrolysis. For some plant materials, enzymes are also added at this stage to induce enzymatic hydrolysis of starch or the polysaccharides present. An example of an enzyme used is alpha-amylase, which catalyzes the hydrolysis of the α-1,4-glycosidic linkage of amylose and amylopectin present in starch and results in the formation of shorter-chain compounds, mainly in the form of dextrins. Proteolytic enzymes are also used for increasing the protein digestibility and extraction efficiency, as well as for improving the suspension stability [9, 15]. Beans can also be subjected to such a process. Alternatively, initial dry grinding of the raw material can be employed, followed by its aqueous extraction at an elevated temperature [9].

The next step in the production of plant-based beverages is the separation of the solid from the liquid fraction, by filtration or centrifugation of the obtained suspension. The resulting plant-based beverage may undergo the standardization process in order to obtain a product with a previously assumed composition, enriched with vitamins or minerals. In the case of bean seeds, subsequent additional heating is carried out to a particular temperature depending on the specificity of the raw material [9, 10, 12].

Usually, ultrahigh temperature (UHT) treatment is applied, where the product is heated in flow to 135–150°C for a few seconds to obtain a commercially sterile one. This process degrades and converts the vegetative forms into microorganisms, while maintaining the taste and aroma of the product. The obtained, microbiologically safe product is poured into unit packages, stored, and distributed [9, 10, 12].

Plant-based beverages exhibit low suspension stability due to the presence of solid particles (e.g., protein, starch, fiber, and other solid residues of plant material). To increase the stability of cow milk substitutes, hydrocolloids of plant origin are added before the final thermal run. Alternatively, the resulting suspension is subjected to homogenization and micronization, which leads to an increase in the stability of the system without the addition of hydrocolloids. This process involves simultaneous grinding and mixing of the particles of the dispersed phase, while forcing the liquid heterogeneous system under high pressure (15–25 MPa) through the homogenizing gap. After micronization, the particle size usually ranges from 0.5 μm to 10 μm. Consequently, the obtained product will have greater creaminess and homogeneity compared to the beverage subjected only to the homogenization process [9, 12].

3. Fermentation of bean-based beverages using lactic acid bacteria and propionic acid bacteria

For many years, attempts have been made to obtain fermented plant-based beverages with the same amount of lactic acid bacteria as in the fermented dairy beverages [16–18]. Several biotechnology companies offer starter cultures for the fermentation of plant products. The addition of these cultures is aimed at obtaining vegan fermented beverages, which are substitutes for milk yogurts. These products most often contain microorganisms that are used for the fermentation of milk, including lactic acid bacteria and bifidobacteria such as *Streptococcus thermophilus*, *Lactobacillus delbrueckii* subsp. *bulgaricus*, *Lactobacillus acidophilus*, *Lactobacillus paracasei*, *Bifidobacterium animalis*, and *Bifidobacterium lactis* [19]. Furthermore, Wajcht's research [14] proves the possibility of using *Propionibacterium freudenreichii* subsp. *shermanii* for the production of fermented bean-based beverages (obtained from germinated adzuki bean and mung bean seeds). After 24-hour fermentation of bean beverages at 37°C, the pH was in the range of 4.3–4.7, and the population of propionibacteria was not lower than 7 log10 CFU/mL [14]. Which proves that *Propionibacterium freudenreichii* subsp. *shermanii* show the ability to grow and ferment sugars contained in bean-based beverages to an extent no worse than the lactic acid bacteria do.

The population size of these microorganisms throughout the shelf life of such beverages is an important factor. It is one of the indicators of the quality and health-promoting properties of these products. The minimum number of cells in such products should be at least 7 log10 CFU/mL or g for starter bacteria and at least 6 log10 CFU/mL or g for additional microorganisms (e.g., probiotics) [20]. It has already been established that the selection of bacteria used for fermentation and the composition and acidity of the product have a significant impact on the viability of the starter and prebiotic bacteria, as well as on the maintenance of the required bacterial population [18, 21]. Ziarno et al. [10] used two commercially available industrial yogurt starter cultures, namely Yo-Mix 205 LYO (DuPont Danisco; consisting of *S. thermophilus*, *L. delbrueckii* subsp. *bulgaricus, L. acidophilus*, and *B. lactis* with sacharose and maltodextrins as carriers) and ABY-3 Probio-Tec (Chr. Hansen; consisting of *S. thermophilus*, *L. delbrueckii* subsp. *bulgaricus*, and documented probiotic strains *L. acidophilus* La-5 and *B. animalis* subsp. *lactis* BB-12), for the fermentation of bean-based beverages obtained from germinated bean seeds of the "Piękny Jaś Karłowy" variety. In the fermented beverages thus obtained, the level of bacteria of the starter culture and additional microorganisms was, respectively, at least 7 log10 CFU/mL and at least 6 log10 CFU/mL. During 28 days of storage at 6°C, there was a significant reduction in the population of *S. thermophilus*, *L. acidophilus*, and *Bifidobacterium* in the beverages; however, the levels of microorganisms were not below 7 log10 CFU/mL and 6 log10 CFU/mL, respectively. Maciejak [12] noted that the population of starter microorganisms was at the level of 8.1 log10 CFU/mL in the bean beverage fermented with the industrial starter culture ABY-3. Zaręba and Ziarno [18] showed that the fermentation of plant-based beverage matrices (soy, rice, and coconut beverages) is more conducive to the development and survival of streptococci compared to lactobacilli. However, the survival rate of both lactobacilli and lactobacilli depends on the type of plant-based beverages and the starter culture used, as well as the degree of fermentation of the beverage (final pH). Therefore, the starter culture should be carefully selected for the specific type of plant beverage, and the storage temperature of the final product should also be adjusted.

4. Nutritional and health value of bean seeds and bean-based beverages

Depending on the variety, white bean seeds contain approximately 21–23 g of total proteins, approximately 0.8–1.6 g of fat, approximately 60–63 g of total carbohydrates, including approximately 40 g of starch and approximately 15–24 g of dietary fiber per 100 g [22–26].

The nutritional and health value of bean beverages depends on the recipe composition and the amount of bean seeds in the product [10, 12, 14, 19, 27]. Ziarno et al. [10] obtained a bean-based beverage by blending 100 g of presoaked white bean seeds of the "Piękny Jaś Karłowy" variety with 900 g of drinking water. Then, the homogenate was boiled to gelatinize the starch contained in the beans. The obtained mixture was filtered through a sieve and sterilized at 121°C for 20 minutes. Among other components, the protein content of the beverage obtained was estimated at 2.3 g/100 g. The study by Jeske et al. [28] reported that commercial plant-based beverages have a comparable protein content.

The main types of proteins found in legume seeds, including bean seeds, are globulins and albumin, which account for 50–70% and 20% of all proteins, respectively [25]. Globulins, which are the dominant fraction of proteins, are referred to as storage proteins. These are stored in membrane-bound organelles, vacuole stores, or protein bodies. In parenchymal cells, globulins survive drying out during seed maturation and undergo proteolysis during germination, providing free amino acids [7, 24, 29, 30].

The storage proteins of bean seeds, like other legumes, have a relatively low content of methionine (approximately 0.1–0.37 g/100 g), cysteine and cystine (0.23–0.25 g/100 g), and also tryptophan (0.25–0.27 g/100 g); however, they are rich in lysine (1.4–1.6 g/100 g), which is the limiting amino acid [26]. Consuming legumes and cereals together in a ratio of 35:65 significantly improves the quality of the supplied protein, making the meal wholesome with a favorable composition of amino acids [7, 24, 29–31].

Most legume seeds, including the white bean ones, contain a maximum of about 5% fat in dry matter (DM), except chickpeas and soybeans, which contain approximately 15% and 47% of fat, respectively [32]. However, in the fermented bean-based beverages prepared by Maciejak [12], the total fat content was 0.16 g/100 g. The fat level in commercial plant beverages is usually regulated (and increased), for example, by the addition of vegetable oils [19]. According to the research of Jeske et al. [28], commercial plant-based beverages have a comparable fat content as the bean-based beverages prepared by Maciejak [12].

The main lipid components of bean seeds are triacylglycerols (TAGs) and phospholipids [33]. The lipid fraction is rich in mono- and polyunsaturated fatty acids (PUFA) (approximately 0.07–0.10 g/100 g and 0.36–0.51 g/100 g, respectively), which constitute approximately 60% of all fatty acids [26, 34]. In some legumes, PUFA are present in the form of linoleic acid (C18:2, included in the omega-6 acid fraction) and α-linolenic acid (C18:3, included in the omega-3 acid fraction). These acids cannot be synthesized by the human body, so they must be constantly supplied in the diet [31]. Among the unsaturated fatty acids, linoleic acid dominates (0.19–0.27 g/100 g), accounting for 21–53% of all fatty acids in beans [24, 29]. The content of linolenic acid is in the range of 026.16–0.23 g/100 g or accounts for 4–22% of the total pool of fatty acids. The seeds of all types of legumes are characterized by a very low content of trans fatty acids, constituting less than 1% [26, 35]. The fat present in legumes does not contain cholesterol [34]. While examining the lipid profile of white bean seeds of the "Piękny Jaś Karłowy" variety, Ziarno et al. [36] showed that the dominant fatty acid was linolenic acid (C18:2 n-6c), amounting to 39.23% of the total pool. Other unsaturated acids present in significant amounts were α-linolenic acid (23.23% of all fatty acids) and oleic acid (17.58% of all fatty acids). The most abundant saturated acids were palmitic acid (12.78% of all fatty acids) and stearic acid (3.68% of all fatty acids). Overall, all unsaturated and saturated acids, respectively, amounted to 81.87% and 18.13% of the total pool of fatty acids. The remaining acids present were about 0.5% or less of all fatty acids. For comparison, Ryan et al. [37] estimated the share of α-linolenic, linoleic, and oleic acid in kidney beans, which amounted to 45.69%, 26.04%, and 11.97% of all fatty acids, respectively. Palmitic acid and stearic acid, respectively, amounted to 14.2% and 1.3% of the total pool. The proportion of unsaturated fatty acids was 83.8% and that of saturated fatty acids was 16.5%. In another work [38], the fatty acid profile was determined for beans (*P. vulgaris*) and other legumes. For common beans, the content of linoleic acid, α-linolenic acid, and oleic acid (C18:1 n-9) was, respectively, 43.1%, 12.4%, and 13.9% of all fatty acids. The following saturated fatty acids were found in the highest content: palmitic C16:0 (16.8% of all fatty acids) and stearic acids C18:0 (3.5% of all fatty acids). In Adzuki bean seeds, the dominant fatty acids were palmitic, stearic, oleic, linoleic, and α-linolenic acids. Of these, unsaturated fatty acids, mainly linoleic, α-linolenic, and oleic acids, were found in large proportions, which constituted from 70.6% to 73.8% of the total content of fatty acids depending on the variety [34]. Another type of legume seeds studied were mung bean seeds, in which the total amount of lipids was 1.2–1.56% of dry weight depending on the cultivar. As in the previous case, the dominant fatty acid was linoleic acid, which was in the range of 340.5–465.7 mg/100 g of dry weight, while there were significant amounts of palmitic, oleic, α-linolenic, and stearic acids as well [39].

In addition, the positional distribution of fatty acids in the TAG molecules has found interest in increasing research works. Significant differences have been observed in the distribution of fatty acids in TAGs depending on the variety of beans and other legume seeds [33, 37, 38, 40, 41]. In his diploma thesis, Ziarno et al. [36] described the positional distribution of fatty acids in the TAG molecules in the lipids of bean seeds of the "Piękny Jaś Karłowy" variety (**Table 1**). Ryan et al. [37] determined the content of α-linolenic, linoleic, and oleic acids in kidney beans to be, respectively, 45.69%, 26.04%, and 11.97% of all fatty acids. Palmitic acid and stearic acid, respectively, amounted to 14.2% and 1.3% of the total pool of fatty acids. Unsaturated fatty acids amounted to 83.8% of all fatty acids, and saturated acids to 16.5%. In another study, Grela and Gunter [38] determined the fatty acid profile for beans (*P. vulgaris*) and other legumes. In common beans, linoleic acid, α-linolenic acid, and oleic acid amounted to 43.1%, 12.4%, and 13.9% of all fatty acids, respectively. Among the saturated fatty acids, palmitic (16.8% of all fatty acids) and stearic (3.5% of all fatty acids) acids were found in the highest content.

For comparison, in Adzuki bean seeds, most of the unsaturated fatty acids (>96% of fatty acids) were accumulated in the sn-2 position of the TAG molecules. Saturated acids were accumulated in the sn-1 and sn-3 positions, except oleic acid, which was accumulated evenly in all three positions [34]. As for the positional distribution of the TAG molecules in broad bean seeds, similarly to Adzuki beans, a significant amount of unsaturated fatty acids (>95% of fatty acids) were accumulated in the sn-2 position. Only oleic acid was found to be almost evenly occupying the sn-1, sn-2, and sn-3 positions. Saturated acids, such as palmitic and stearic

Type of fatty acid	TAG content of fatty acid [% of fatty acids]	Content of fatty acid [% of fatty acids] in position		Content of fatty acid in the sn-2 position [% of fatty acids]
		sn-2	sn-1,3	
Palmitic (C16:0)	12.78	8.68	14.83	22.63
Stearic (C18:0)	3.68	2.16	4.44	19.55
Oleic (C18:1 n-9c)	17.58	16.79	17.97	31.83
Linoleic (C18:2 n-6c)	39.23	46.52	35.59	39.53
α-Linolenic (C18:3 n-3c)	23.23	22.67	23.51	32.53

Table 1.
Positional distribution of fatty acids in triacylglycerol (TAG) molecules in the lipids of the white bean seeds of the "Piękny Jaś Karłowy" variety (based on [36]).

acids, were accumulated in the sn-1 and sn-3 positions. An almost identical distribution was noted in peas, where more than 90% of unsaturated fatty acids were accumulated in the sn-2 position, while saturated acids were mainly accumulated in the sn-1 and sn-3 positions [33, 40, 41].

The carbohydrates contained in legume seeds, including bean seeds, are mainly composed of starch, fiber, nonstarch polysaccharides, and nondigestible oligosaccharides, which together constitute 30–40% of the dry weight of seeds in the case of species with a high protein content (e.g., lupines and soybeans) or 50–65% of DM in those containing less protein in seeds [25, 42]. However, in the obtained unfermented bean beverages, Cichońska [19] determined a total carbohydrate content of 1.8–3.7 g/100 g depending on the production recipe used.

Bean seeds contain more than 40% of starch and 10–25% of dietary fiber [26]. They are also rich in the resistant fraction of starch, which is not hydrolyzed in the small intestine but is fermented by colonic microorganisms at different rates [7]. The ratio of soluble fiber to insoluble fiber is similar to that found in cereals, which is approximately 1:3 [35]. Consumption of bean fiber is associated with many health and physiological benefits, including improvement in the metabolism of glucose and lipids [24, 43]. When resistant starch in beans is fermented, short-chain fatty acids (such as acetic, butyric, and propionic acid) are produced, the concentration and distribution of which depend on the microorganisms and the carbohydrate content in the gut. Therefore, resistant starch is often considered a prebiotic component as it can regulate the amount and activity of the intestinal flora. It is a precursor of butyrates, which are known for their anti-inflammatory and anticancer properties [44]. In addition, resistant starch binds with bile acids, lowers the absorption of cholesterol and fat, and reduces the absorption of glucose. It also influences the acceleration and regulation of intestinal peristalsis, prevents constipation, and supports the development of beneficial microflora in the large intestine. Furthermore, it reduces hunger and increases satiety after a meal, as it swells in the stomach [24, 43].

Consuming legume seeds, including bean seeds, can cause gas production due to bacterial fermentation, including undigested leftovers. The main oligosaccharide found in legumes is raffinose, which is attributed to the properties of a prebiotic (fermented by probiotic bacteria to short-chain fatty acids); thus, legumes can improve colon health and reduce the risk of colon cancer [31].

Proper preparation of bean beverages can reduce the content of nonenzymatically decomposed ingredients in the human digestive tract [10, 13, 14]. Studies have shown that when lactic acid bacteria are used for the fermentation of legume seeds, the level of stachyose is reduced, which in turn reduces digestive discomfort and flatulence [45–49]. Maciejak [12] obtained fermented and unfermented bean beverages from the germinated white bean seeds of the "Piękny Jaś Karłowy" variety (**Table 2**). Their data showed a significant reduction in the content of all analyzed saccharides. For instance, the content of sucrose was reduced by 82.46%, and raffinose content reached 82.84%. The content of stachyose after the fermentation process was reduced by 68.64%, while the smallest change, amounting to 60.61%, was recorded for verbascose.

Of all the seeds of legumes, beans have the highest content of minerals. They can act as an important source of iron (7–11 mg/100 g), zinc (3–4 mg/100 g), copper (0.6–1.0 mg/100 g), phosphorus (300–450 mg/100 g), and potassium (1500–1800 mg/100 g) in the daily diet [23, 24, 26, 50, 51]. Although the content of minerals varies depending on the variety of beans [23, 24], the seeds of white beans are identified as a source of calcium (170–240 mg/100 g) and magnesium (180–190 mg/100 g) [26, 44]. In bean-based beverages, the content of minerals is

Bean beverages	Sacharose [mg/g]	Raffinose [mg/g]	Stachyose [mg/g]	Verbascose [mg/g]
Nonfermented	1.725 ± 0.601	0.425 ± 0.177	2.725 ± 0.015	0.15 ± 0.071
Fermented with lactic acid bacteria	0.303 ± 0.086	0.073 ± 0.019	0.855 ± 0.219	0.059 ± 0.058

Table 2.
Content of selected carbohydrates in the bean-based beverage obtained from the germinated white bean seeds of the "Piękny Jaś Karłowy" variety (based on [12]).

determined by the recipe composition, especially the amount of bean seeds in the products.

Legume seeds, including beans, are also a good source of water-soluble vitamins, such as B vitamins [10, 26, 52]. White bean seeds contain thiamine (0.4–0.7 mg/100 g), riboflavin (0.1–0.2 mg/100 g), niacin (0.5–1.4 mg/100 g), and acid folic (370–390 μg/100 g) [26, 52]. Similar to minerals, the content of vitamins varies depending on the variety of beans [23, 24]. Legume seeds, including bean seeds, are deficient in fat-soluble vitamins and vitamin C [26]. The vitamin content of bean-based beverages is also determined by the recipe composition, in particular the amount of bean seeds in such products, as well as by the thermal (pasteurization, sterilization) and enzymatic (germination, fermentation) treatments used. Although, Zhang et al. [53] showed that in fortified oat beverages subjected to UHT treatment by direct steam injection, the content of vitamins A, D3, K, B6, B12, thiamine, riboflavin, niacin, and folic acid was not influenced by the thermal process. In addition, the UHT sterilization of the bean-based beverage had a similar effect on the vitamins mentioned. Ziarno et al. [10] showed that the unfermented bean-based beverages obtained from bean seeds of the "Piękny Jaś Karłowy" variety contained 0.69 mg/kg thiamine, 0.20 mg/kg riboflavin, 2.34 mg/kg niacin, and 0.55 mg/kg pyridoxine.

An interesting group of compounds present in legume seeds, including bean seeds, are active biological substances, such as phytochemicals and antioxidants. These include polyphenols, lignans, isoflavonoids, protease inhibitors, trypsin and chymotrypsin inhibitors, saponins, alkaloids, phytoestrogens, and phytates [31, 53–55]. Most of them are referred to as antinutritional ingredients. Although they are nontoxic substances, they can cause physiological side effects affecting the digestion of proteins or the bioavailability of certain minerals. However, many of them show a different, positive biological activity [31, 53]. The polyphenol content in beans depends, among others, on the species, cultivar, and agrotechnical and climatic conditions of cultivation [30, 56]. Due to the high content of polyphenolic compounds, such as tannins, flavonoids, isoflavonoids, phenolic acids, phytates, or lignans, legume seeds, including bean seeds, are known for their anticancer properties [24, 29, 30, 50, 57]. These properties of beans are especially related to the presence of protease inhibitors, which help to naturally regulate the levels of inhibitors found in the human body. Antioxidant components also influence the anticarcinogenic properties of beans. A proper diet, including bean seeds, helps to prevent cancer, while in people with advanced-stage cancer, it can support oncological therapy. Furthermore, beans have a high content of hemagglutinins and lectins that direct atypical cells to the apoptotic pathway [30, 57, 58]. The content of these bioactive substances in bean seeds also depends, among others, on species, cultivar, and agrotechnical and climatic conditions of cultivation [56]. In the case of bean-based beverages, the polyphenol content is influenced by many factors, mainly the recipe composition and technological activities used in the production process [19, 59]. In addition, the content of these bioactive substances in beverages is influenced by the various technological processes used during the initial processing of bean seeds and the processing of the prepared product (germination, blending, mixing, homogenization, pasteurization or sterilization, oxygenation) [59–61].

Legume seeds, including bean seeds, are characterized by a low glycemic index (<55), and can therefore limit hyperglycemia [52]. They can contribute to reducing the risk of type 2 diabetes and control the levels of sugars and lipids in the human body [24, 29, 35, 50]. In people with type 2 diabetes, increased consumption of beans can reduce tissue insulin similarity [30, 62]. Consuming legumes four times a week or more may also reduce the risk of coronary heart disease by 22%. Increased consumption of legume seeds contributes to lowering the levels of total cholesterol and low-density lipoprotein cholesterol [42]. Moreover, bioactive compounds, such as isoflavonoids or lignans, present in legumes may play a role in the prevention of osteoporosis [44].

5. Influence of germination on the quality of bean-based beverages

Legumes contain many antinutritional ingredients, such as trypsin inhibitors, phytic acid, or α-galactosides, as well as indigestible carbohydrates; therefore, they must be subjected to appropriate treatments before consumption [11, 63]. Methods such as dehulling, heating, germination, fermentation, soaking, or partial hydrolysis using proteolytic enzymes can be applied. These improve the quality of seeds and increase their nutritional quality [64–66]. The optimal time of these processes is determined as 3–5 days, and they should be performed at room temperature [10, 12, 67].

Germination is one of the most important and effective processes that can improve the nutritional value of seeds, by increasing the content of certain nutrients (e.g., proteins or polyphenols) or eliminating undesirable components (e.g., trypsin inhibitors, stachyose, raffinose) [10, 12, 36, 68]. During this process, all lipolytic, amylolytic, and proteolytic enzymes are activated, which catalyze the breakdown of storage substances, respiratory processes, and the synthesis of macromolecular compounds needed for the growing parts of the embryo [69]. Germinated bean seeds are characterized by a lower level of stachyose and raffinose but a higher content of polyphenols and protein [64, 65, 70]. Proteolytic enzymes help in the breakdown of endosperm proteins, while dipeptides, tripeptides, and new embryonic proteins are synthesized simultaneously [69].

The lipid content and fatty acid profile of legume seeds, including bean seeds, also change during the germination process [36, 71, 72]. Frias et al. [68] found that the germination process carried out for 9 days led to an increase in the inhibition of lipid oxidation. On the other hand, Ziarno et al. [36] showed that in the bean seeds of the "Piękny Jaś Karłowy" variety, the germination process significantly reduced the oxidative stability of the fat isolated from the seeds. Compared to raw beans, the researcher recorded an almost fourfold reduction in the time of oxidation. The maximum oxidation time of raw beans was 44.93 minutes, while for a beverage made from the germinated bean seeds, the oxidation time was only 11.82 minutes.

Moreover, during the germination process of legume seeds, including bean seeds, the content of phenolic compounds [69] has been found to be significantly increased. In the research on lupine seeds, the germination process was found to increase the content of α-tocopherol (from 0.19 mg/100 g DM in the control to 3.91 mg/100 g DM after 9 days of germination) and decrease the content of γ-tocopherol (from 20.1 mg/100 g DM in the control to 13.4 mg/100 g DM after 9 days of germination), but it did not significantly affect the content of δ-tocopherol (0.22 mg/100 g DM in the control compared to 0.25 mg/100 g DM after 9 days of germination). Additionally, a significant increase in the content of vitamin C was found (from 6.48 mg/100 g DM in the control to 56.1 mg/100 g DM after 9 days of germination). Germinated lentil or chickpea seeds were also characterized by an increase in the bioavailability of calcium (respectively 29.3% and 19.3% in the control and 46.5% and 32.9% in germinated seeds) and iron (respectively 10.2% and 11.3% in the control and 18.5% and 18.6% in germinated seeds) [73].

The use of various technological and biological procedures (e.g., soaking, cooking, germination, fermentation) also greatly influences the fatty acid profile of legume seeds, including bean seeds [36, 74, 75]. Germination increases the availability of free amino acids and vitamins. It also improves the content and digestibility of proteins as well as the content of crude fiber [76]. Furthermore, germination of legume seeds, including bean seeds, partially minimizes the activity of trypsin inhibitors, and eliminates flatulence caused by oligosaccharides from the raffinose family [11]. This contributes not only to significant biochemical and nutritional changes but also to sensory changes in legumes [10, 12, 14, 59, 63, 77].

The influence of germination on other substances such as bioactive compounds and antinutritional ingredients has also been investigated [10, 67, 69, 78]. The antinutritional ingredients present in materials of plant origin include e.g., protease inhibitors, phytates, glucosinolates, saponins tannins, lectins, oligosaccharides and non-starch polysaccharides, phytoestrogens, alkaloids, antigenic compounds, gossypols, cyanogens, cyclopropenoid fatty acids, and antivitamins. Meanwhile, the identified bioactive compounds can be divided into six categories, namely flavonoids, phenolic acids, saponins, alkaloids, polysaccharides and others (i.e., (e.g., terpenoids, stilbene glycosides, coumarins). Valdes et al. [56] showed that bean germination may affect the accumulation of polyphenols in black bean sprouts. The researchers observed a 1.54-fold increase in polyphenol content in bean sprouts after 6 days of bean fermentation. Other studies [64, 65] indicated that after 5 days of bean seed germination, the content of polyphenols increased from 2.28 mg/g DM to 2.95 mg/g DM, whereas there was a reduction in the content of raffinose (from 5.90 mg/g DM to 1.98 mg/g DM) and stachyose (from 60.28 mg/g DM to 5.87 mg/g DM).

Some researchers reported that the germination process influenced the level of B vitamins in legume seeds [53]. The direction of these changes was dependent on the cultures and processing parameters [10, 79–81]. El-Adawy [82] showed a significant increase in riboflavin content (from 1.733 g/kg DM to 2.013 g/kg DM) and a slightly lower increase in pyridoxine content (from 4.663 g/kg DM to 4.830 g/kg DM) after 3 days of germination of chickpea seeds. In addition, there was a significant reduction in the content of thiamine (from 4.533 g/kg DM to 2.833 g/kg DM) and niacin (from 16.027 g/kg DM to 15.186 g/kg DM). Ziarno et al. [10] observed a significant reduction in the content of riboflavin, niacin, and pyridoxine in bean-based beverages fermented with yogurt bacteria.

6. Effect of fermentation on the quality of bean-based beverages

Another process that can improve the nutritional value of legumes, including bean seeds, is fermentation. A wide range of microorganisms can be involved in the fermentation of legume seeds as follows: lactic acid bacteria of the genera *Lactobacillus*, *Leuconostoc*, *Pediococcus*, and *Enterococcus*; molds of the genera *Rhizopus*, *Aspergillus*, and *Mucor*; yeasts of the genera *Saccharomyces* and *Zygosaccharomyces*; or bacteria of the genus *Bacillus* [12, 14, 18, 83, 84]. Fermentation reduces the level of antinutritional substances, increases digestibility, and enhances the level of valuable nutrients [10, 12, 14, 59, 77, 85–92]. Spontaneous fermentation is quite widespread, especially in developing countries. However, this technology has disadvantages such as low efficiency, variable product quality, and safety drawbacks [89]. One of the alternatives is controlled fermentation with the use of lactic acid bacteria, which can be used for different raw materials, not only legumes but also cereals and root crops [18, 93–95].

Lactic acid fermentation has been used for years for obtaining fermented beverages. For the production of fermented foods, starter cultures of known composition are used, which allows reproducibility of the process [83, 91, 96]. Moreover, such products become a source of bioactive substances and prebiotic substances, which are extremely important for health (β-glucan, oligosaccharides, and resistant starch), as well as live cells of lactic acid bacteria and probiotic strains. This also applies to nondairy fermented beverages [12, 14, 18, 90–92]. The most popular types of bacteria used for fermentation purposes, which also exhibit probiotic properties, are lactic acid bacteria *Lactobacillus, Bifidobacterium* and *Propionibacterium* [12, 14, 97, 98].

Fermentation does not significantly affect the protein content of bean seeds, although an increase in the content of exogenous amino acids has been noted after the process, especially in leucine (from 7.98 mg/g to 16.68 mg/g), threonine (from 4.16 mg/g to 7.31 mg/g), and isoleucine (from 4.26 mg/g to 6.39 mg/g) [64, 65, 99]. Similar observations were made with regard to other legume seeds. In broad bean seeds, fermentation with the use of a *Lactobacillus plantarum* strain caused an increase in the content of free amino acids (from 7.10 g/kg to 17.66 g/kg), mainly essential amino acids and γ-aminobutyric acid. The protein digestibility improved to a small but statistically significant extent (from 75.1% to 76.6%) [100]. Furthermore, protein digestibility improved in vivo (3.5%) as well as *in vitro* (12.55%) [48]. Similarly, Czarnecka et al. [101] used *L. plantarum* for the fermentation of bean seeds and found a significant improvement in the *in vitro* digestibility of protein (from 59.1% to 72.2%).

A slight reduction in fat content was also observed in fermented bean seeds, probably due to the hydrolysis of fatty acids [64–66]. This is evidenced by the effect of fermentation using different bacterial cultures of *S. thermophilus* and *L. delbrueckii* subsp. *bulgaricus* on the fatty acid profile [36, 72, 102]. Ziarno et al. [36] showed in the white bean seeds of the "Piękny Jaś Karłowy" variety that the combined processes of germination and fermentation with lactic acid bacteria of the genus *Lactobacillus* contributed to an increase in the amounts of saturated acids (palmitic and stearic) and oleic acid in fatty acid profile compared to raw beans. However, the direction of changes depended on the selection of the *Lactobacillus* strain for fermentation of the bean-based beverage. The dominant fatty acid in the fatty acid profile of raw bean seeds was linolenic acid, which constituted 39.23% of the total fatty acid pool. Other unsaturated acids that were present in a significant amount were α-linolenic (23.23% in fatty acid profile) and oleic (17.58% in fatty acid profile) acids. The most abundant saturated acids were palmitic acid (12.78% in fatty acid profile) and stearic acid (3.68% in fatty acid profile). Overall, the total amount of all unsaturated acids was 81.87% in the fatty acid profile of raw bean seeds, and that of saturated acids was 18.13%. The remaining acids were present at about 0.5% or less in the total pool. On the other hand, in bean-based beverages fermented by variants of the *Lactobacillus* genus, an increase in the content of palmitic acid (except for the beverage fermented by a strain of *L. plantarum*) and stearic acid, compared to raw beans, was noted. Moreover, in fermented bean-based beverages, an increase in the content of oleic acid and a decrease in the content of PUFA (i.e., linoleic acid and α-linolenic acid) were observed. However, Barampama and Simard [103] obtained contrasting results in their work. They used *L. plantarum* to ferment beans. After 16 hours of fermentation at 37°C, they observed a reduction in the content of stearic acid (from 12.20 mg/100 g to 120.6 mg/100 g), palmitic acid (from 124.22 mg/100 g to 118.57 mg/100 g), oleic acid (from 56.39 mg/100 g to 52.39 mg/100 g), linoleic acid (from 130.97 mg/100 g to 113.26 mg/100 g), and linolenic acid (from 137.69 mg/100 g to 110.34 mg/100 g).

The combination of the germination and fermentation processes also affects the positional distribution of fatty acids in the middle (sn-2) and external (sn-1,3) positions in bean seeds. The differences in the amount of individual fatty acids in the middle position (sn-2) were found to be statistically insignificant [36]. In the current literature, there is only limited information on the impact of various biological and technological processes on the positional distribution of fatty acids in the TAG molecules present in legume seeds, including bean seeds. One study assessed the effect of microwave heating on the distribution of fatty acids in the hypocotyl TAGs of two soybean seeds. It was found that after 12 minutes or more of heating, there were minor but statistically significant changes in the distribution of fatty acids. These changes were manifested, inter alia, as an increase in the percentage of palmitic acid in the sn-1 and sn-3 positions and a reduction in the percentage of linoleic acid in the sn-2 position [104].

In the fermented bean seeds, changes in the content of complex carbohydrates, such as stachyose, raffinose, and verbascose, were found, but the degree of reduction in their concentration depended on the type of microorganisms used in the process [48, 64, 65, 101]. Germination and fermentation by lactic acid bacteria (LAB) or bifidobacteria increased the amount of simple sugars in the beans, while they induced the breakdown of raffinose and stachyose into galactose, glucose, sucrose, and fructose [13]. Ziarno et al. [10] showed that the fermented beverages produced from germinated white bean seeds of the "Piękny Jaś Karłowy" variety using two yogurt starter cultures contained about 31% and 17% of stachyose and raffinose, respectively, compared to those before the fermentation (2.73 mg/kg and 0.43 mg/kg, respectively), but the reduction in verbascose was not significant. As a result of germination, maltose was released from complex carbohydrates contained in beans [69, 105]. Granito and Alvarez [48] showed an increase in the content of resistant starch by about 13% and in the content of available starch by about 35%, as well as a decrease in the content of soluble (by over 63%) and insoluble fiber (by 39%). Czarnecka et al. [101] showed an improvement in *in vitro* starch digestibility in beans by 55–58% after germination.

Fermentation with LAB and bifidobacteria may also change the content of B vitamin group, but the direction of these changes is dependent on the cultures and processing parameters that influence the biosynthesis of these vitamins [10, 79–81, 106, 107]. In addition, fermentation contributes to the reduction of antinutritional components. The content of polyphenols was also shown to be increased by 43.4%, whereas the content of non-nutrients such as tannins was reduced (by approximately 84%) [64, 65]. Fermentation with the fungus *Rhizopus oligosporus* was found to cause an almost threefold increase in the content of polyphenols and a twofold increase in their antioxidant activity [99]. In the bean seeds fermented with the fungus of the genus *Rhizopus*, an increase in the content of polyphenols by 43.4% and a reduction in the content of non-nutrients such as tannins (by approximately 84%) were found [64, 65]. In broad beans fermented with *L. plantarum* bacteria, a reduction in the activity of trypsin inhibitors by approximately 56% and a reduction in the content of condensed tannins by approximately 50% were found [100].

7. Conclusions

Use of the germination and fermentation processes in combination in the production of fermented beverages from the seeds of ordinary beans has not been discussed in the scientific literature so far. This chapter presents various studies proving that it is possible to obtain fermented bean-based beverages using these processes together, and the health and nutritional values of these beverages are higher than that of raw bean seeds. The most promising results were reported for the lactic acid fermentation of bean-based beverages, which yields wholesome nondairy products with similar quality as their dairy counterparts. The use of lactic acid bacteria has a positive effect on the digestibility of fermented beverages, owing to the reduction of oligosaccharides that cause digestive discomfort. Most importantly, the obtained fermented bean-based beverages are ideal for the survival of the starter bacterial cells during both fermentation and refrigerated storage, and therefore, they can be considered as functional products acting as a carrier for probiotics.

Acknowledgements

This work was supported by a grant from Warsaw University of Life Sciences - WULS-SGGW.

Conflict of interest

Authors have declared that they do not have any conflict of interest for publishing this research.

Author details

Anna Veber[1], Dorota Zaręba[2] and Małgorzata Ziarno[3]*

1 Department of Food and Biotechnology, Faculty of Agrotechnological, Federal State Budgetary Educational Institution of Higher Education, Omsk State Agrarian University named after P.A. Stolypin, Russia

2 Technical School of Gastronomy in Warsaw, Warsaw, Poland

3 Department of Food Technology and Assessment, Institute of Food Sciences, Warsaw University of Life Sciences, Warsaw, Poland

*Address all correspondence to: malgorzata_ziarno@sggw.edu.pl

References

[1] Korus J, Gumul D, Achramowicz B. Chemical composition of five new kidney bean (*Phaseolus vulgaris* L.) cultivars. Żywność. Nauka. Technologia. Jakość 2005;4:81-86. (in Polish, Abstract in English)

[2] Broughton WJ, Hernandez G, Blair M, Beebe S, Gepts P, Vanderleyden J. Beans (*Phaseolus* spp.) - model food legumes. Plant and Soil 2003;252:55-128. DOI: 10.1023/A:1024146710611

[3] Nowosielski J, Nowosielska D, Frak M, Jankiewicz U, Bulińska-Radomska Z. Using AFLP method to compare and evaluate of genetic diversity of selected varieties and landraces of common bean (*Phaseolus vulgaris* L.) and bean (*Phaseolus coccieneus* L.). Acta Scientiarum Polonorum. Biotechnologia 2011;1:5-16. (in Polish, Abstract in English)

[4] Teixeria-Guedesa C, Oppolzerc D, Barrosc A, Pereira-Wolsona C. Impact of cooking method on phenolic composition and antioxidant potential of four varieties of *Phaseolus vulgaris* L. and *Glycine max* L., LWT- Food Science and Technology 2019;103:238-246. DOI: 10.1016/j.lwt.2019.01.010

[5] Messina M, Soy foods, isoflavones, and the health of postmenopausal women. The American Journal of Clinical Nutrition 2014;100:423S–430S. DOI: 10.3945/ajcn.113.071464

[6] Stasiak A, Ulanowska A. Entioxidant activity of the new bean cultivars (*Phaseolus vulgaris* L.). Żywność. Nauka. Technologia. Jakość 2008;1:74-82. (in Polish, Abstract in English)

[7] Krupa-Kozak U. Main nutritional and antinutritional compounds of bean seeds - a rewiev. Polish Journal of Food and Nutrition Sciences 2008;58:149-155.

[8] Martínez R, López-Jurado M, Wanden-Berghe C. Beneficial effects of legumes on parameters of the metabolic syndrome: a systematic review of trials in animal models. British Journal of Nutrition 2016;116:402-424. DOI: https://doi.org/10.1017/S0007114516001963

[9] Mäkinen OE, Wanhalinna V, Zannini E, Arendt EK. Foods for special dietary needs: Non-dairy plant based milk substitutes and fermented dairy type products. Critical Reviews in Food Science and Nutrition 2015;56:339-349. DOI: 10.1080/10408398.2012.761950

[10] Ziarno M, Zaręba D, Maciejak M, Veber AL. The impact of dairy starter cultures on selected qualitative properties of functional fermented beverage prepared from germinated white kidney beans. Journal of Food and Nutrition Research 2019;2:167-176. ISSN: 1338-4260

[11] Adil Nawaz M, Tan M, Øiseth S, Buckow R. An Emerging Segment of Functional Legume-Based Beverages: A Review, Food Reviews International 2020. DOI: 10.1080/87559129.2020.1762641

[12] Maciejak M. Dairy cultures application in production of dry bean (*Phaseolus vulgaris* L.) fermented beverage. Warsaw: Warsaw University of Life Sciences. [thesis]. 2017. (in Polish, Abstract in English)

[13] Radzikowski R. Influence of germination and fermentation processes on the content of carbohydrates in beans. Warsaw: Warsaw University of Life Sciences. [thesis]. 2019. (in Polish, Abstract in English)

[14] Wajcht M. Research on the use of *Propionibacterium* sp. in the production of fermented milk and vegetable drinks.

Warsaw: Warsaw University of Life Sciences. [thesis] 2019. (in Polish, Abstract in English)

[15] Swati S, Tyagi SK, Anurag RK. Plant-based milk alternatives an emerging segment of functional beverages: a review. Journal of Food Science and Technology 2016;53:3408-3423. DOI: 10.1007/s13197-016-2328-3

[16] Farnworth ER, Mainville I, Desjardins MP, Gardner N, Fliss I, Champagne C. Growth of probiotic bacteria and bifidobacteria in a soy yogurt formulation. International Journal of Food Microbiology 2007;116:174-181. DOI: 10.1016/j.ijfoodmicro.2006.12.015

[17] Champagne CP, Green-Johnson J, Raymond Y, Barrette J, Buckley N. Selection of probiotic bacteria for the fermentation of a soy beverage in combination with *Streptococcus thermophilus*. Food Research International 2009;42:612-621. DOI: 10.1016/j.foodres.2008.12.018

[18] Zaręba D, Ziarno M The viability of yogurt bacteria in selected plant beverages. Zeszyty Problemowe Postępów Nauk Rolniczych 2017;591:87-96. DOI 10.22630/ZPPNR.2017.591.46

[19] Cichońska P. The analysis of selected physico-chemical characteristics of a buckwheat-bean beverage. Warsaw: Warsaw University of Life Sciences. [thesis]. 2020. (in Polish, Abstract in English)

[20] CXS 243-2003. Standard for Fermented Milks. Adopted in 2003. Revised in 2008, 2010, 2018. Codex Alimentarius FAO/WHO [Internet]. 2020. Available from: http://www.fao.org/fao-who-codexalimentarius/sh-proxy/en/?lnk=1&url=https%253A%252F%252Fworkspace.fao.org%252Fsites%252Fcodex%252FStandards%252FCXS%2B243-2003%252FCXS_243e.pdf [Accessed: 2020-09-02]

[21] Zaręba D, Ziarno M, Obiedziński M. Viability of yoghurt bacteria and probiotic strains in models of fermented and non-fermented milk. Medycyna Weterynaryjna 2008;64:1007-1011. (in Polish, Abstract in English).

[22] Roe M, Finglas P, Church S. The Composition of Foods, Food Standards Agency 2003;6:250-253

[23] Kapusta F. Legumes as protein source for humans and animals. Engineering Sciences and Technologies 2012,1:16-32. (in Polish, Abstract in English).

[24] Hayat I, Ahmad A, Masud T, Ahmed A, Bashir S. Nutritional and health perspectives of beans (*Phaseolus vulgaris* L.): an overview. Critical Reviews in Food Science and Nutrition 2014;54:580-592. DOI: 10.1080/10408398.2011.596639

[25] De Ron AM. Grain Legumes. Springer-Verlag New York; 2015. 438 p. DOI: 10.1007/978-1-4939-2797-5

[26] FoodData Central. U.S. Department of Agriculture. Agricultural Research Service. [Internet]. 2020. Available from: https://ndb.nal.usda.gov/index.html [Accessed: 2020-09-02]

[27] Cichońska P. The research on consumer preferences regarding the consumption of cereal beverages and developing the recipe for a millet beverage. Warsaw: Warsaw University of Life Sciences. [thesis]. 2018. (in Polish, Abstract in English)

[28] Jeske S, Zannini E, Arendt EK. Evaluation of Physicochemical and Glycaemic Properties of Commercial Plant-Based Milk Substitutes. Plant Foods for Human Nutrition 2017;72:26-33. DOI 10.1007/s11130-016-0583-0

[29] Messina V. Nutritional and health benefits of dried beans. The American Journal of Clinical Nutrition 2014;100:437-332. DOI: 10.3945/ajcn.113.071472

[30] Wawryka J, Zdrojewicz Z. Bean – an important element of a healthy diet. Nutritional values analysis, Pediatria i Medycyna Rodzinna 2016;12:394-403. DOI: 10.15557/PiMR.2016.0039 . (in Polish, Abstract in English)

[31] Maphosa Y, Jideani VA. The Role of Legumes in Human Nutrition. In: Edited by Chávarri Hueda M. Functional Food - Improve Health through Adequate Food. Intech; 2017. p. 103-121. DOI: 10.5772/intechopen.69127

[32] Messina MJ. Legumes and soybeans: overview of their nutritional profiles and health effects. The American Journal of Clinical Nutrition 1999;70:439-450. DOI: 10.1093/ajcn/70.3.439s

[33] Yoshida H, Tomiyama Y, Mizushina Y. Characterization in the fatty acid distributions of triacyloglicerols and phospholipids in kidney beans (*Phaseolus vulgaris* L.). Journal of Food Lipids 2005;12:169-180. DOI: 10.1111/j.1745-4522.2005.00016.x

[34] Yoshida H, Tomiyama Y, Yoshida N, Shibata K, Mizushina Y. Regiospecific profiles of fatty acids in triacylglycerols and phospholipids from adzuki beans (*Vigna angularis*) Nutrients 2010;2:49-59. DOI: 10.3390/nu20100049

[35] Bouchenak M, Lamri-Senhadji M. Nutritional quality of legumes, and their role in cardiometabolic risk prevention: a review. Journal of Medical Food 2013;16: 1-14. DOI: 10.1089/jmf.2011.0238

[36] Ziarno M, Bryś J, Parzyszek M, Veber A.L. Effect of lactic acid bacteria on the lipid profile of bean-based plant substitute of fermented milk. Microorganisms 2020;8;1348. DOI: 10.3390/microorganisms8091348

[37] Ryan E, Galvin K, O'Connor TP, Maguire AR, O'Brien NM. Phytosterol, squalene, tocopherol content and fatty acid profile of selected seeds, grains, and legumes. Plant Foods for Human Nutrition 2007;65:85-91. DOI: 10.1007/s11130-007-0046-8

[38] Grela ER, Gunter KD. Fatty acid composition and tocopherol content of some legume seeds. Animal Feed Science and Technology 1995;52:325-331

[39] Anwar F, Latif S, Przybylski R, Sultana B, Ashraf M. Chemical composition and antioxidant activity of seeds of different cultivars of mungbean. Journal of Food Science 2007;72:503-510. DOI: 10.1111/j.1750-3841.2007.00462.x

[40] Yoshida H, Saiki M, Yoshida N, Tomiyama Y, Mizushina Y. Fatty acid distribution in triacylglycerols and phospholipids of broad beans (*Vicia faba*). Food Chemistry 2009;112:924-928. DOI: 10.1016/j.foodchem.2008.07.003

[41] Yoshida H, Tomiyama Y, Tanaka M, Mizushina Y. Distribution of fatty acids in triacylglycerols and phospholipids from peas (*Pisum sativum* L.). Journal of the Science of Food and Agriculture 2007;87:2709-2714. DOI: 10.1002/jsfa.3035

[42] Rebello CJ, Greenway FL, Finley JW. A review of the nutritional value of legumes and their effects on obesity and its related co-morbidities. Obesity Reviews 2014;15:392-407. DOI: 10.1111/obr.12144

[43] Trinidad TP, Mallillin AC, Loyola AS, Sagum RS, Encabo RR. The potential health benefits of legumes as a good source of dietary fibre. British Journal of Nutrition 2010;103:569-574. DOI: 10.1017/S0007114509992157

[44] Gebrelibanos M, Tesfaye D, Raghavendra Y, Sintayeyu B. Nutritional and health implications of legumes. International Journal of Pharmaceutical Sciences and Research 2013;4:1269-1279. DOI: 10.13040/IJPSR.0975-8232.4(4).1269-79

[45] Duszkiewicz-Reinhard W, Gujska E,., Khan K. Reduction of stachyose in legume flours by lactic acid bacteria. Journal of Food Science 1994;59:115-117. DOI: 10.1111/j.1365-2621.1994.tb06911.x

[46] Wang YC, Yu RC, Yang HY, Chou CC. Sugar and acid contents in soymilk fermented with lactic acid bacteria alone or simultaneously with bifidobacteria. Food Microbiology 2003;20:333-338. DOI: 10.1016/S0740-0020(02)00125-9

[47] LeBlanc JG, Silvestroni A, Connes C, Juillard V, de Giori GS, Piard JC, Sesma F. Reduction of non-digestible oligosaccharides in soymilk: application of engineered lactic acid bacteria that produce alpha-galactosidase. Genetics and Molecular Research 2004;3:432-440

[48] Granito M, Alvarez G. Lactic acid fermentation of black beans (*Phaseolus vulgaris*): microbiological and chemical characterization. Journal of the Science of Food and Agriculture 2006;86:1164-1171. DOI: 10.1002/jsfa.2490

[49] Granito M, Champ M, Guerra M, Frias J. Effect of natural and controlled fermentation on flatus-producing compounds of beans (*Phaseolus vulgaris*). Journal of the Science of Food and Agriculture 2003;83:1004-1009. DOI: 10.1002/jsfa.1388

[50] Polak R, Phillips EM, Campbell A. Legumes: Health Benefits and Culinary Approaches to Increase Intake. Clinical Diabetes 2015;33:198-205. DOI: 10.2337/diaclin.33.4.198

[51] Safaeiyan A, Pourghassem-Gargari B, Zarrin R. Randomized controlled trial on the effects of legumes on cardiovascular risk factors in women with abdominal obesity. ARYA Atheroscler 2015;11:117-125.

[52] Mlynekova Z, Chrenkova M, Formelova Z. Cereals and legumes in nutrition of people with celiac disease. International Journal of Celiac Disease 2014;2:105-109. DOI: 10.12691/ijcd-2-3-3

[53] Zhang H, Önning G, Triantafyllou AÖ, Öste R. Nutritional Properties of Oat-based Beverages as Affected by Processing and Storage. Journal of the Science of Food and Agriculture 2007;87:2294-2301. DOI: 10.1002/jsfa.2987.

[54] Zieliński H. Low molecular weight antioxidants in the cereal grains – a review. Polish Journal of Food and Nutrition Sciences 2002;52:3-9.

[55] Szajdek A, Borowska J. Antioxidant properties of plant-based food products. Żywność. Nauka. Technologia. Jakość 2004;4:5-28. (in Polish, Abstract in English)

[56] Thomas-Valdés S, Medeiros Coelho C, Michelluti D, Cardoso Garcıa Tramonte V. Association of genotype and preparation methods on the antioxidant activity, and antinutrients in common beans (*Phaseolus vulgaris* L.). LWT-Food Science and Technology 2011;44:2104-2111. DOI: 10.1016/j.lwt.2011.06.014

[57] Piecyk M, Klepacka M, Worobiej E. The content of trypsin inhibitors, oligosccharides, and phytic acid in the bean seed (*Phaseolus vulgaris*) preparations obtained by crystallization and classical isolation, Żywność. Nauka. Technologia. Jakość 2005;3:92-104. (in Polish, Abstract in English)

[58] Custódio ID, Marinho Eda C, Gontijo C. Impact of chemotherapy on diet and nutritional status of women with breast cancer: a prospective study. PLoS One 2016;11:124-126. DOI: 10.1371/journal.pone.0157113

[59] Dzierzgowska O. Research on the production of functional ice cream based on beans fermented by lactic acid bacteria. Warsaw: Warsaw University of Life Sciences. [thesis]. 2019. (in Polish, Abstract in English)

[60] Remiszewski M, Kulczak M, Przygoński K, Korbas E, Jeżewska M. Effect of extrusion on antioxidant activity of selected legume seeds. Żywność. Nauka. Technologia. Jakość 2007;2:98-104. ISSN : 1425-6959 (in Polish, Abstract in English)

[61] Yang Q, You Gan R, Ge Y, Zhang D, Corke H. Polyphenols in Common Beans (*Phaseolus vulgaris* L.): Chemistry, Analysis, and Factors Affecting Composition. Comprehensive Reviews in Food Science and Food Safety 2018;17:1518-1539. DOI: 10.1111/1541-4337.12391

[62] Dhillon PK, Bowen L, Kinra S. Legume consumption and its association with fasting glucose, insulin resistance and type 2 diabetes in the Indian Migration Study. Public Health Nutrition 2016;19:3017-3026. DOI: 10.1017/S1368980016001233

[63] Lopez-Amoros ML, Hernandez T, Estrella I.. Effect of germination on legume phenolic compounds and their antioxidant activity. Journal of Food Composition and Analysis 2006;19:277-283. DOI: 10.1016/j.jfca.2004.06.012

[64] Bieżanowska-Kopeć R, Pisulewski PM, Polaszczyk S. Effect of water-thermal processing on the content of bioactive compounds in common bean (*Phaseolus vulgaris* l.) seeds. Żywność. Nauka. Technologia. Jakość 2006;2:82-92. (in Polish, Abstract in English)

[65] Bieżanowska-Kopeć R, Pisulewski PM. The effect of thermal and biological processing on antioxidant activity of common bean seeds (*Phaseolus vulgaris* L.). Żywność. Nauka. Technologia. Jakość 2006;3:51-64. (in Polish, Abstract in English)

[66] Adebowale OJ, Maliki K. Effect of fermentation period on the chemical composition and functional properties of Pigeon pea (*Cajanus cajan*) seed flour. International Food Research Journal 2011;18:1329-1333.

[67] Xue Z, Wang C, Zhai L, Yu W, Chang H, Kou X, Zhou F. Bioactive compounds and antioxidant activity of mung bean (*Vigna radiata* L.), soybean (*Glycine max* L.) and black bean during the germination process. Czech Journal of Food Science 2016;34:68-78. DOI: 10.17221/434/2015-CJFS

[68] Frias J, Miranda ML, Doblado R, Vidal-Valverde C. Effect of germination and fermentation on the antioxidant vitamin content and antioxidant capacity of *Lupinus albus* L. var. *Multolupa*. Food Chemistry 2005;92:211-220. DOI: 10.1016/j.foodchem.2004.06.049

[69] Lewicki PP. Sprouts as source of valuable nutritients. Żywność. Nauka. Technologia. Jakość 2010;6:18-33. DOI: 10.15193/zntj/2010/73/018-033 (in Polish, Abstract in English)

[70] Bubelová Z, Sumczynski D, Salek RN. Effect of cooking and germination on antioxidant activity, total polyphenols and flavonoids, fiber content, and digestibility of lentils (*Lens culinaris* L.). Journal of Food Processing and Preservation 2018;42:e13388. DOI: 10.1111/jfpp.13388

[71] Shah SA, Zeb A, Masood T, Nareen N, Abbas SJ, Samiullah M,

Alim MA, Muhammad A. Effects of sprouting time on biochemical and nutritional qualities of mungbean varieties. African Journal of Agricultural Research 2011;6:5091-5098. DOI: 10.5897/AJAR11.480

[72] Zaręba D. Fatty acid profile of soya milk fermented by various bacteria strains of lactic acid fermentation. Żywność Nauka Technologia Jakość 2009;16:59-71. (in Polish, Abstract in English)

[73] Ghavidel RA, Prakash J. The impact of germination and dehulling on nutrients, antinutrients, *in vitro* iron and calcium bioavailability and *in vitro* starch and protein digestibility of some legume seeds. LWT - Food Science and Technology 2007;40:1292-1299. DOI: 10.1016/j.lwt.2006.08.002

[74] Abdel-Rahman EA, El-Fishawy FA, El-Geddawy MA, Kurz T, El-Rify MN. The changes in the lipid composition of mung bean seeds as affected by processing methods. International Journal of Food Engineering 2007;3:article 6 . DOI: 10.2202/1556-3758.1186

[75] Megat-Rusydi MR, Noraliza CW, Azrina A, Zulkhairi A. Nutritional changes in germinated legumes and rice varieties. International Food Research Journal 2011;18:705-713.

[76] Kavitha S, Parimalavalli R. Effect of processing methods on proximate composition of cereal and legume flours. Journal of Human Nutrition & Food Science 2014;2:1051.

[77] Kostański P. Research on obtaining high-protein functional ice cream based on fermented beans. Warsaw: Warsaw University of Life Sciences, [thesis], 2019. (in Polish, Abstract in English)

[78] Guajardo-Flores D, Serna-Saldıvar S, Gutierrez-Uribe J. Evaluation of the antioxidant and antiproliferative activities of extracted saponins and flavonols from germinated black beans (*Phaseolus vulgaris* L.). Food Chemistry 2013;141:1497-1503. DOI: 10.1016/j.foodchem.2013.04.010

[79] Vidal-Valverde C, Frias J, Sierra I, Blazquez I, Lambein F, Kuo Y.H. New functional legume foods by germination: effect on the nutritive value of beans, lentils and peas. European Food Research and Technology 2002;215:472-477. DOI: 10.1007/s00217-002-0602-2

[80] Nkhata SG, Ayua E, Kamau EH, Shingiro JB. Fermentation and germination improve nutritional value of cereals and legumes through activation of endogenous enzymes. Food Science & Nutrition 2018;6(8):2446-2458. DOI: 10.1002/fsn3.846

[81] Hou JW, Yu RC, Chou CC. Changes in some components of soymilk during fermentation with bifidobacteria. Food Research International 2000;33:393-397. DOI: 10.1016/S0963- 9969(00)00061-2.

[82] El-Adawy TA. Nutritional composition and antinutritional factors of chickpeas (*Cicer arietinum* L.) undergoing different cooking methods and germination. Plant Foods for Human Nutrition 2002;57: 83-97. DOI: 10.1023/A:1013189620528

[83] Tamang JP, Watanabe K, Holzapfel WH. Review: diversity of microorganisms in global fermented foods and beverages. Frontiers in Microbiology 2016;7:377. DOI: 10.3389/fmicb.2016.00377

[84] Reddy NR, Pierson MD, Salunkhe DK. Legume Based Fermented Foods. Routledge Revivals. CRC Press, 2018, 262 p. ISBN 1315894904, 9781315894904

[85] Starzyńska-Janiszewska A, Stodolak B, Mickowska B. Effect of

controlled lactic acid fermentation on selected bioactive and nutritional parameters of tempeh obtained from unhulled common bean (*Phaseolus vulgaris*) seeds. Journal of the Science of Food and Agriculture 2014;94(2):359-366. DOI: 10.1002/jsfa.6385

[86] Pandey A. Solid-state fermentation. Biochemical Engineering Journal 2003;13:81-84. DOI: 10.1016/S1369-703X(02)00121-3

[87] Starzyńska-Janiszewska A, Stodolak B. Effect of inoculated lactic acid fermentation on antinutritional and antiradical properties of grass pea (*Lathyrus sativus* 'Krab') flour. Polish Journal of Food and Nutrition Sciences 2011;61:245-249. DOI: 10.2478/v10222-011-0027-3

[88] Subramaniyam R, Vimala R. Solid state and submerged fermentation for the production of bioactive substances: a comparative study. International Journal of Science and Nature 2012;3:480-486.

[89] Onwurafor EU, Onweluzo JC, Ezeoke AM. Effect of fermentation methods on chemical and microbial properties of mung bean (*Vigna radiata*) Flour. Nigerian Food Journal 2014;32:89-96. DOI: 10.1016/S0189-7241(15)30100-4

[90] Vasudha S, Mishra H. Non-dairy probiotic beverages. International Food Research Journal 2013;20:7-15. ISSN (Online): 2231 7546

[91] Waters DM, Mauch A, Coffey A, Arendt EK, Zannini E. Lactic acid bacteria as a cell factory for the delivery of functional biomolecules and ingredients in cereal-based beverages: a review. Critical Reviews in Food Science and Nutrition 2015;55:503-520. DOI: 10.1080/10408398.2012.660251

[92] Lorenzo P, Zannini E, Arendt EK. Lactic acid bacteria as sensory biomodulators for fermented cereal-based beverages. Trends in Food Science & Technology 2016;54:17-25. DOI: 10.1016/j.tifs.2016.05.009

[93] Wajcht M. Impact of AGM Innotec starter cultures on the quality features of fermented dairy and plant beverages. [thesis]. Warsaw: Warsaw University of Life Sciences. 2020. (in Polish, Abstract in English)

[94] Kowalska E, Ziarno M. The possibility of obtaining buckwheat beverages fermented with lactic acid bacterial cultures and bifidobacteria. Foods 2020;9(12);1771. DOI: 10.3390/foods9121771

[95] Wang C, Liang S, Wang H, Guo M. Physiochemical properties and probiotic survivability of symbiotic oat-based beverage. Food Science and Biotechnology 2018;27:735-743. DOI: 10.1007/s10068-017-0290-0

[96] Marco ML, Heeney D, Binda S, Cifelli CJ, Cotter PD, Foligné B, Ganzle M, Kort R, Pasin G, Philanto A, Smid EJ, Hutkins R. Health benefits of fermented foods: microbiota and beyond. Current Opinion in Biotechnology 2017;44:94-102. DOI: 10.1016/j.copbio.2016.11.010

[97] Marsh A J, Hill C, Ross RP, Cotter PD. Fermented beverages with health-promoting potential: past and future perspectives. Trends in Food Science and Technology 2014;38:113-124. DOI: 10.1016/j.tifs.2014.05.002

[98] Ranadheera CS,Vidanarachchi JK, Rocha RS, Cruz AG, Ajlouni S. Probiotic Delivery through Fermentation: Dairy vs. Non-Dairy Beverages. Fermentation 2017;3:67. DOI: 10.3390/fermentation3040067

[99] Miszkiewicz H, Okrajni J, Bielecki S. Changes in the content and anti-oxidative activity of polyphenols and albumins in pea during its fermentation in an SSSR bioreactor.

Żywność. Nauka. Technologia. Jakość 2008;3:67-79. (in Polish, Abstract in English)

[100] Coda R, Melama L, Rizello CG, Curiel JA, Sibakov J, Holopainen U, Pulkkinen M, Sozer N. Effect of air classification and fermentation by *Lactobacillus plantarum* VTT E-133328 on faba bean (*Vicia faba* L.) flour nutritional properties. International Journal of Food Microbiology 2015;193:34-42. DOI: 10.1016/j.ijfoodmicro.2014.10.012

[101] Czarnecka M, Czarnecki Z, Nowak J, Roszyk H. Effect of lactic fermentation and extrusion of bean and pea seeds on nutritional and functional properties. Nahrung 1998;42:7-11. DOI: 10.1002/(SICI)1521-3803(199802)42:01<7::AID-FOOD7>3.0.CO;2-I

[102] Enujiugha VN. Nutrient changes during the fermentation of African oil bean (*Pentaclethra macrophylla* benth) seeds. Pakistan Journal of Nutrition 2003;2:320-323. DOI: 10.3923/pjn.2003.320.323

[103] Barampama Z, Simard RE. Effects of soaking, cooking and fermentation on composition, in-vitro starch digestibility and nutritive value of common beans. Plant Food for Human Nutrition 1995;48:349-365. DOI: doi: 10.1007/BF01088494

[104] Yoshida H, Kanei S. Tomiyama Y, Mizushina Y. Regional distribution in the fatty acids of triacylglycerols and phospholipids within soybean seeds (*Glycine max* L.). European Journal of Lipid Science and Technology 2006;108(2): 149-158. DOI: 10.1002/ejlt.200500248

[105] Adamidou S, Nengas I, Grigorakis K, Nikolopoulou D, Jauncey K. Chemical Composition and Antinutritional Factors of Field Peas (*Pisum sativum*), Chickpeas (*Cicer arietinum*), and Faba Beans (*Vicia faba*) as Affected by Extrusion Preconditioning and Drying Temperatures. Cereal Chemistry 2011;88(1):80-86. DOI: 10.1094/CCHEM-05-10-0077

[106] Champagne CP, Tompkins TA, Buckley ND, Green-Johnson JM. Effect of fermentation by pure and mixed cultures of *Streptococcus thermophilus* and *Lactobacillus helveticus* on isoflavone and B-vitamin content of a fermented soy beverage. Food Microbiology 2010;27: 968-972. DOI: 10.1016/j.fm.2010.06.003

[107] LeBlanc JG, Laino JE, Juarez del Valle M, Vannini V, van Sinderen D, Taranto MP, Font de Valdez G, Savoy de Giori G, Sesma F. B-Group vitamin production by lactic acid bacteria – current knowledge and potential applications. Journal of Applied Microbiology 2011;111:1297-1309. DOI: 10.1111/j.1365-2672.2011.05157.x

Chapter 7

Use of Soy Milk in Lamb Feeding

Youssouf Toukourou and Abdoulaye Moubarack

Abstract

Soy milk was administered to *Djallonké* Lambs in pre weaning. Three groups of 20 animals, all from a traditional farming, were performed. Group 1 (control) was deprived of soy milk. In the 2nd and 3rd group lambs received 50 and 100 ml soy milk respectively per head. Food supplementation with soy milk began a week after the lambs' birth. Soy milk was administered daily at the same time in one meal using a suckling bottle before leaving to the pasture. The results showed a significant delay of growth of the control group compared to the other groups. At the end of the 2nd week, the body weight difference was in average 0.32and 0.42 kg respectively for the control and the two other groups. At the end of the 12th week this difference became 2.55 and 3.22 kg respectively for the control and the two other groups. No significant differences were observed between the live weights' mean in the 2nd and 3rd group.

Keywords: growth, soy milk, food, *Djallonké* lambs, Benin

1. Introduction

The nutritional importance of animal protein in the diet is well established. However, it is becoming increasingly difficult to make this food in sufficient quantity available to the populations, especially in developing countries. Yet these countries have sufficient local resources that can be better harnessed to meet the food and nutritional needs of their populations. The transformation, by animals, of primary plant resources into animal proteins with high nutritional value for humans remains the most effective means of ensuring populations a healthy and balanced diet. To this end, small ruminants, sheep and goats, represent a real opportunity for poor rural populations to improve the availability of food resources of animal origin. Indeed, these animal species are relatively easy to breed and therefore easily adapt to the socio-economic conditions of rural households. Despite these adaptive qualities and a strong aptitude for reproduction (view video in annex) (precocious puberty, good prolificacy, non-seasonal sexual cycle) [1], the milk yield of local breeds of small ruminants and in particular that of sheep in Benin remains low. This yield is estimated at 57.44 kg and 86.44 kg, for a lactation period of 105 days and 112 days, respectively for ewes with one and two lambs [2]. By crossing this level of milk production of ewes with the nutritional need for maintenance of lambs, which is estimated at 421 kj/kg of metabolizable weight [3], it is clearly seen that the lambs are being fed well below their physiological requirements. Indeed, such milk performance, obviously, does not adequately cover the nutritional needs of two, sometimes three lambs per birth, during the lactation period. Due to the low

IntechOpen

milk production of females, young animals in pre-weaning fail to fully express their growth potential [4]. This results in sometimes chronic undernourishment leading to difficulties in the growth of young animals and a predisposition to diseases. The high mortality of lambs is therefore the main factor in the drop in productivity and varies according to the authors between 20 to 48% [3–6] and decreases (5 to 20%) after weaning and in adult animals [7]. To obtain better growth performance from young lambs during the suckling period, it is essential that the nutritional requirements at this stage of life are sufficiently covered. The ideal feed for this, at least during the first two weeks of lambs life, is sufficient natural sheep's milk. Other sources of milk, such as cow's milk or formula made from specific plant material can be used. Various plant products are used for the manufacture of milk drinks. These milk drinks represent for most people, an alternative to natural animal milk, because they do not support lactose, a sugar naturally contained in the milk of mammals. Plant milks also have the advantage of being rich in vitamins and minerals. These milks also contain unsaturated fats, which is more beneficial for health, as they do not contain cholesterol, like the saturated fats found in animal milk. Plant milks produced from legumes, such as soybeans, also contain essential amino acids that are essential for growth. Plant milks are rarely used in animal feed. In developed countries, where cows produce enough milk, its use in animal feed is very widespread. [8] investigated the possibility of raising lambs with milk replacer from cow's milk. [9] used soy milk to supplement pre-weaning lambs. The choice of using cow's milk to supplement the feed of pre-weaning lambs nevertheless poses the problem of availability and accessibility of this foodstuff under farming conditions in Benin. This milk comes mainly from extensive traditional breeding characterized by very low production [10]). This small quantity of milk is usually shared between man and calf which, as a result, cannot adequately cover its nutritional needs and therefore does not manage to fully express its growth potential. To mitigate the consequences of low local milk production, Benin regularly resorts to the massive importation of milk and dairy products. This strategy is proving too costly for a very low income country. Multiple livestock development projects involving the importation of reputed dairy breeds have not made it possible to permanently resolve this problem. However, Benin has diversified natural resources that can be developed. This is the case, among other things, with soy, which is a legume whose food and nutritional properties are highly appreciated [11]. This crop, well adapted to the climatic conditions of Benin, is widely practiced by agro-pastoralists. Rural households use soybeans for making cheese [12] which is perfectly anchored in the eating habits of the populations. Soy is also used in many countries for the manufacture of various foods and drinks commonly known as soy milk [13, 14]. It also finds wide use in animal feed, especially in the manufacture of feeds for monogastrics. Soybeans transformed into milk can be used as an alternative for this purpose to remedy the nutritional deficit of young animals during the lactogenic phase and at the same time contribute to freeing part of the milked milk for human consumption. The research question that emerges from this reflection is whether soy milk can enable *Djallonké* lambs to fill the food and nutritional deficit caused by the low milk production of the ewes during the suckling period.

2. Material and methods

2.1 Study environment

The animal material, object of the present study, is located in Tourou, a city district of the commune of Parakou located in the center of Benin between

19° 21 'North latitude and 2° 36' East longitude. With an average altitude of 350 m, it extends over an area of 441 km^2 of which about 30 km^2 are urbanized. There is a Sudano-Guinean type climate with an average annual rainfall that varies between 1000 mm and 1500 mm and two seasons which alternate as follows: a rainy season which extends from mid-April to mid-October, and a dry season from mid-October to mid-April. Temperatures in this part of Benin oscillate between 28 and 35° C. The vegetation cover observed in Parakou is dominated by wooded and grassy savannah. Vegetation is abundant during the rainy season and good quality fodder resources are thus available for animal feed.

2.2 Period and duration of the test

The trial was conducted during the rainy season for a period of 3 months. The vegetation cover at that time was luxuriant and offered ruminants an abundant forage availability.

2.3 Preparation and administration of soy milk

The preparation of the soya milk administered to the lambs was carried out from seeds cultivated and marketed in Ouaké, a locality in Benin located about 172 km north of the study site. The soy milk used was obtained by mixing 1 kg of whole soya beans, previously cleaned, with 8 liters of water. After 24 hours of soaking, the seeds, once rinsed, are poured into two liters of water and then mixed using a kitchen Moulinex. The resulting mixture was mixed with six liters of water and then boiled for 30 minutes. After cooking, the resulting porridge was filtered using a very fine mesh sieve to separate the soy milk from the residual mass. Soymilk was fed to the lambs at a temperature of 38° C every morning at the same time as a single meal using suckling bottles.

2.4 Animal material

The animal material used in the present study consists of 60 lambs (27 males and 33 females) of the Djallonké breed from 47 ewes, most of them multiparous. The animals, of which 34 were from a single birth and 26 from a double birth, came from ewes in traditional extensive herds (**Figure 1**). The animals are left to stray during the day and are tied to stakes in the evening when they return from pasture. By the age of 1 month all the lambs had received prophylactic treatment with Oxycline 20%, anti-diarrheal treatment and a vitamin complex by intramuscular injection. Three batches of lambs distributed at random were made. Lot 1 (control) is deprived of soy milk. The lambs of batches 2 and 3 received, from one week of age, respectively a supplement of 50 ml and 100 ml of soy milk.

2.5 Measurement and data collection

The data collected, recorded and analyzed during the present study focused mainly on the nutritional quality of soy milk, the quantity of soy milk served, refused and consumed, as well as on the live weight of the lambs. A sample of 500 g of soy milk was taken every four weeks and analyzed (**Table 1**). These analyzes made it possible to determine the chemical composition of soy milk according to official methods approved by the AOAC [5]. The measurement of the total amount of carbohydrate was estimated by subtracting the various nutrients: water, total nitrogen, fat, and crude ash from the original substance. The estimation of the gross energy of soy milk was carried out by considering that 1 g of carbohydrate and

Figure 1.
Djallonké sheep herd in Benin.

Nutrients	Soy milk during the test period			Ewe's milk*
	1st month	2nd month	3rd month	
Dry matter (%)	9.19 ± 1.11	9.02 ± 1.26	9.43 ± 1.09	16.47
Total Nitrogenous Matter (%)	5.93 ± 1.16	5.90 ± 1.39	5.88 ± 1.06	5.37
Fat (%)	2.38 ± 0.77	2.16 ± 0.32	2.70 ± 0.62	6.02
Crude ash (%)	0.38 ± 0.07	0.47 ± 0.10	0.41 ± 0.10	0.77
Carbohydrate (%)	0.50 ± 0.02	0.49 ± 0.01	0.44 ± 0.01	—
Gross energy (kcal /100 g)	48.02 ± 6.13	45.86 ± 6.47	50.48 ± 6.66	108

**Source: [2].*

Table 1.
Nutritional value of soy milk during the test period compared to whole sheep milk.

protein respectively release 4.1 kcal and that 1 g of fat releases 9.1 kcal [5]. The soy milk was administered individually every morning at the same time between 8 and 10 a.m. before leaving for the pasture. Likewise, individual weighing are carried out weekly on an empty stomach on the lambs and the corresponding weights are recorded on individual monitoring sheets.

3. Results

3.1 Chemical composition and nutritional value of soy milk

The nutritional values of soya milk, compared to that of sheep's milk, are shown in **Table 1**. These values show that the soymilk manufacturing process remained broadly unchanged throughout the test. However, it emerges from this comparison that the soya milk used in the present study had a much lower dry extract, fat and crude ash content than ewe's milk. The total nitrogen content was slightly higher in soy milk than in ewe's milk [6]. Therefore, soy milk has a gross energy between 45.86 kcal and 50.48 kcal per 100 g of product. It was found to be significantly less energetic than sheep's milk estimated at 108 kcal (**Table 1**).

3.2 Lamb weight growth

The body live weights of the lambs during the test period are shown in **Table 2**. At the end of the first week of testing, the lambs displayed an average body live weight of 2.34 kg, 2.40 kg and 2.36 kg respectively for lots 1, 2 and 3. At the end of the first week of testing, the lambs displayed an average live weight of 2.34 kg, 2.40 kg and 2.36 kg respectively for lots 1, 2 and 3. At the second week, the lambs of the control group, deprived of soya milk, displayed an average live weight of 0.32 and 0.42 kg significantly ($p < 0.001$) lower than those of groups 2 and 3 supplemented respectively with 50 ml and 100 ml of soy milk. The difference in live weight between the lambs in lots 2 and 3 was not significant ($p > 0.05$). This difference in weight growth between the batch of control animals and the two other batches was significantly ($p < 0.001$) accentuated and was located at 1.28 kg and 1.65 kg respectively for batches 2 and 3 at the 6th week. At the end of the experiment, at thirteen weeks of age, i.e. twelve weeks of soy milk treatment, the animals averaged a live weight of 6.01 kg, 8.56 kg and 9.23 kg respectively for lots 1 (control), 2 and 3 with a significant difference ($p < 0.001$) between lot 1 and the others. No significant difference ($p > 0.05$) could be noted between lots 2 and 3 throughout the experiment.

Apart from the level of soy milk consumption, other variables involved in the statistical analysis model had a more or less significant influence on the weight

Trial period (weeks)	Treatments (Soy milk consumption)								
	Lot 1 (control: 0 ml)			Lot 2 (50 ml)			Lot 3 (100 ml)		
	N	μ (kg)	SE	N	μ (kg)	SE	N	μ (kg)	SE
1	20	2.34^a	0.04	20	2.40^a	0.04	20	2.36^a	0,04
2	20	2.78^a	0.10	20	3.10^b	0.10	20	3.20^b	0,09
3	20	3.14^a	0.11	20	3.74^b	0.12	20	3.84^b	0,11
4	20	3.42^a	0.14	20	4.28^b	0.15	20	4.40^b	0,14
5	20	3.67^a	0.17	20	3.80^b	018	20	5.03^b	0,16
6	20	4.02^a	0.18	20	5.30^b	0.19	20	5.67^b	0,18
7	20	4.31^a	0.21	20	5.78^b	0.22	20	6.16^b	0,20
8	20	4.61^a	0.22	20	6.26^b	0.23	20	6.74^b	0,21
9	20	4.95^a	0.23	20	6.77^b	0.24	20	7.34^b	0,22
10	20	5.29^a	0.24	20	7.33^b	0.24	20	7.97^b	023
11	20	5.61^a	0.25	20	7.93^b	0.26	20	8.55^b	0,24
12	20	6.01^a	0.26	20	8.56^b	0.27	20	9.23^b	0,25

Values with the same letters superscript on the same line are not significantly different at the 5% level.

Table 2.
Live weight of Djallonké lambs supplemented with soy milk in pre weaning.

Trial period (weeks)	Treatments (Soy milk consumption)											
	Lot 1 (control: 0 ml)				Lot 2 (50 ml)				Lot 3 (100 ml)			
	Single birth		Double birth		Single birth		Double birth		Single birth		Double birth	
	μ (kg)	SE	μ (kg)	SE	μ (kg)	SE	μ (kg)	SE	μ (kg)	SE	μ (kg)	SE
1	2.35^{a}	0.05	2.33^{a}	0.07	2.42^{a}	0.05	2.37^{a}	0.07	2.44^{a}	0.07	2.28^{a}	0.05
2	2.71^{a}	0.11	2.84^{a}	0.15	3.19^{b}	0.12	3.01^{a}	0.16	3.38^{b}	0.15	3.01^{a}	0.12
3	3.20^{a}	0.14	3.09^{a}	0.18	$3,87^{b}$	0.14	3.61^{a}	0.20	4.12^{b}	0.18	3.55^{a}	0.14
4	3.54^{a}	0.17	3.29^{a}	0.22	4.43^{bc}	0.17	4.13^{bc}	0.24	4.71^{b}	0.22	4.09^{c}	0.17
5	3.76^{a}	0.20	3.58^{a}	0.27	5.10^{b}	0.20	4.51^{b}	0.29	5.44^{d}	0.26	4.61^{bc}	0.21
6	4.06^{a}	0.22	3.97^{a}	0.29	5.74^{b}	0.22	4.86^{c}	0.31	6.28^{d}	0.29	5.06^{c}	0.23
7	4.34^{a}	0.25	4.28^{a}	0.33	6.20^{b}	0.25	5.35^{b}	0.36	6.76^{c}	0.33	5.56^{b}	0.26
8	4.66^{a}	0.26	4.57^{a}	0.35	6.70^{b}	0.27	5.83^{b}	0.38	7.40^{c}	0.34	6.08^{b}	0.27
9	5.01^{a}	0.27	4.90^{a}	0.36	7.12^{b}	0.28	6.43^{b}	0.39	8.02^{c}	0.36	6.67^{b}	0.28
10	5.40^{a}	0.29	5.18^{a}	0.39	7.64^{b}	0.29	7.01^{b}	0.41	8.65^{c}	0.38	7.28^{b}	0.30
11	5.77^{a}	0.30	5.45^{a}	0.40	8.28^{b}	0.31	7.57^{b}	0.43	9.27^{c}	0.39	7.84^{b}	0.31
12	6.16^{a}	0.31	5.86^{a}	0.42	8.85^{b}	0.32	8.26^{b}	0.45	9.94^{c}	0.41	8.52^{b}	0.32

Values with the same letters superscript on the same line are not significantly different at the 5% level.

Table 3.
Live weight of Djallonké lambs supplemented with soy milk during the suckling period depending on the mode of birth.

growth of the lambs during the study. Thus, sex significantly ($p < 0.001$) influenced the mean live weight of lambs at the very start of the experiment. Its influence resulted in higher weights in males than in females after a week of testing. Thus, for all the lambs, the average live weight at one week of testing was 2.46 kg for the males and 2.27 kg for the females. Mode of birth as well as birth weight also had a significant influence ($p < 0.05$) on the weight growth of lambs. While the significant influence ($p < 0.001$) of birth weight was already evident from the start of the experiment, that of mode of birth began a little later in the second week, especially in lambs born from a simple birth, and persisted until the end of the experiment.

The results obtained and presented in **Table 3** showed that at the end of the first week of testing, the supplementation of soy milk had no significant effect ($p > 0.05$) on the live weights of the lambs whatever the mode of birth. The significant effect of supplementing soymilk was evident from the second week of the test. At this time, single born control lambs, with an average live weight of 2.71 kg, showed on average a significant growth retardation ($p < 0.001$) of 0.48 and 0.67 kg respectively vis-à-vis lambs born single from lots 2 and 3. This growth retardation was only 0.17 kg between the twin control lambs and those from the other two lots from the same birth mode during the same period. After four weeks of testing, the weight loss in single born control lambs was 0.89 kg and 1.17 kg, respectively, compared to single born lambs in lots 2 and 3. In twin lambs, this delay from the control batch, although significant, was less pronounced and amounted to 0.84 kg and 0.80 kg respectively compared to batches 2 and 3. At the end of the experiment at twelve weeks of testing, this difference in live weight amounted to 2.69 kg and 3.78 kg respectively for the simple birth mode and to 2.4 kg and 2.66 kg for the double birth mode.

3.3 Average daily gain of lambs

The results of the average daily gains are shown in **Table 4**. Overall, consumption of soy milk resulted in average daily gains (ADG) in lambs directly proportional to the level of consumption of soy milk.

After one month of testing, the animals displayed ADGs of 59.76 g, 90.84 g and 95.25 g respectively for batches 1, 2 and 3. Lambs from the control group had a significantly lower average daily growth ($p < 0.001$) than those from groups 2 and 3. Supplementation of 100 ml of soy milk in the lambs from batch 3 did not induce a significantly ($p > 0.05$) more accelerated growth rate compared to their congeners from batch 2 who received 50 ml. At weaning at 3 months, the ADG of the lambs was 50 g, 83 g and 89 g respectively for lots 1, 2 and 3. The difference in ADG between the control batch, which did not receive soy milk, and the other batches was still significant ($P < 0.05$).

Trial period (month)	Treatments (Soy milk consumption)								
	Lot 1 (control: 0 ml)			Lot 2 (50 ml)			Lot 3 (100 ml)		
	N	μ (g)	SE	N	μ (g)	SE	N	μ (g)	SE
1	20	59.76^{a}	4.99	20	90.84^{b}	5.29	20	95.25^{b}	4,90
2	20	42.50^{a}	4.75	20	71.21^{b}	5.03	20	83.86^{b}	4,66
3	20	50.05^{a}	3.95	20	82.83^{b}	4.18	20	89.40^{b}	3,88

Values with the same letters superscript on the same line are not significantly different at the 5% level.

Table 4.
Average daily gain of Djallonké lambs supplemented with soy milk during the suckling period.

3.4 Lamb mortality

No case of mortality was recorded, neither among the control lambs nor among those which benefited from a feed supplement with soya milk, throughout the trial. The sanitary arrangements made at the start of the experiment, namely a prophylactic treatment based on Oxycline 20%, an anti-diarrheal treatment and an intramuscular injection of vitamin complex certainly contributed to obtaining such a result.

4. Discussion

Soy milk as a feed supplement was accepted by Djallonkés lambs in pre-weaning from the second week of life. Soymilk as a dietary supplement at the start of the breastfeeding period could not differentiate between the live weights of the Djallonkés lambs who benefited from it and those who did not. Obviously, natural ewe's milk has proven at this stage of the animals' life to be a food perfectly suited to their physiological needs. Studies have shown that sufficient ewe's milk is necessary to ensure rapid and steady growth in lambs during lactation [14]. The chemical composition of ewe's milk with particularly high dry matter, protein, fat and lactose contents, compared to goat's and cow's milk [15], clearly illustrates its nutritional quality for pre-weaning lambs. The early introduction of formula milk, such as soy milk, was ineffective in improving the weight growth of Djallonke lambs. However, it should be noted that the chemical composition of the soy milk administered to the lambs in the present study is far from meeting their nutritional requirements. Compared to sheep's milk, soy milk in the present study is clearly deficient in energy, particularly in protein and fat, two nutrients which contribute to the energy coverage of lambs. Improving the nutritional quality of soymilk could allow lambs to better express their growth potential. A special formulation of soymilk that takes into account the nutritional requirements of lambs can improve its effectiveness for this purpose. As the lambs got older, the effect of supplementation with soy milk became noticeable on their weight growth, especially between the lambs from the control lot (lot 1) on one side and those from the lots 2 and 3, with 50 ml and 100 ml respectively, on the other. Lambs from the control group, which did not receive soy milk as a feed supplement, were significantly retarded in their growth, compared to their congeners from lots 2 and 3. However, it emerges from the shape of weight growth curve, that from the sixth week, the weight difference between the animals in groups 2 and 3 became more and more visible although not significant ($p > 0.05$). The 50 ml difference in soy milk consumption between lots 2 and 3 was probably not enough to induce a substantial difference in their average live weight. [16] cited by [2] obtained for its part an average live weight of Djallonké lambs located between 6.61 and 7.13 kg at twelve weeks of age at the Okpara Farm, located in the Commune of Kika, 15 km from the city of Parakou, Benin. Tests carried out in the station also enabled [6] to determine live weights of 5.1 and 10.9 kg respectively on the 30th and 90th day in Djallonké lambs. These results are slightly higher than those obtained during the present study for the lambs of the control group. This is most certainly explained by the fact that animals reared in stations have benefited from better breeding conditions than their counterparts reared in a real environment.

For the same amount of soy milk consumed, lambs from a single birth tend to grow faster than those from a double birth. The difference in weight between lambs in lots 2 and 3, although not significant ($p > 0.05$), is more marked in singles than in twins. This suggests that lambs born single tend to benefit more from soy milk than their double born counterparts. [3] confirmed that insufficient milk feeding in Djallonké lamb could retard the weight growth of lambs from a double birth.

At the end of the eighth week of the trial, a slight decrease in ADG was recorded in all batches of animals, regardless of feed level. Lambs at this stage of life are probably out of the accelerated phase of their growth. [17] observed a similar evolution in station in Djallonkés lambs in pre-weaning. The trend between the different lots remained nevertheless maintained with a slightly more accentuated gap between lots 2 and 3. The soymilk rationing imposed on lambs in the present study, combined with an eight-week pre-weaning limitation period, partly explains the average weight growth performance recorded. It is not excluded that an ad libitum supplementation based on soy milk over a regularly breastfeeding period of twelve weeks, improves the weight performance recorded.

5. Conclusion

The use of soy milk as a dietary supplement during the pre-weaning period has proved to be a promising strategy to improve the weight performance of Djallonkés lambs in the commune of Parakou in Benin. The consumption of soy milk allowed the Djallonkés lambs to better express their growth potential. A quantity of 50 ml of soy milk in addition to natural sheep's milk was sufficient for the Djallonkés lambs to significantly improve their growth performance. Beyond this quantity, the Djallonkés lambs continued to improve their growth performance, although not significant.

Author details

Youssouf Toukourou* and Abdoulaye Moubarack
University of Parakou, Parakou, Republic of Benin

*Address all correspondence to: ytoukourou@gmail.com

References

[1] Osuagwuh A I A, Akpokodje J U. An outbreak of abortion in West African Dwarf Goats due to malnutrition . 1986

[2] Amégée Y. Etude de la production laitière de la brebis Djallonké en relation avec la croissance des agneaux. Rev. Elev. Med. v&. Pavs trop. 37 (3): 1984. p. 311-335

[3] ARC Agricultural Research Council. The Nutrient Requirements of Ruminant Livestock. Technical Review by an Agricultural Research Council Working Party, Common wealth Agricultural Bureau, Farnham Royal, UK (1980)

[4] Vallerand F, Branckaert R. La race ovine Djallonké au Cameroun. Potentialités zootechniques, conditions d'élevage, avenir. Revue. Elev. Méd. Vét. Pays trop., 28, 1975. P. 523-545.

[5] Strutz C, Glombitza K F. Les moutons Djallonké élevés par les villageois au Congo, peuvent-ils être sélectionnés pour l'augmentation du poids ? *Rev. Elev. Méd. Vét. Pays Trop.*, **39**, 1986. P. 107-111

[6] Filius P, Weniger J H, Teuscher T. Untersuchungen über die Nutzleistung des Djallonkeschafes; Ein Beitrag zur Kenntnis einer westafrikanischen Schafrasse. Journal of animal breeding and genetic. DOI: 10.1111/j.1439-0388. tb00706.x. Volume 102, Issue 1-5 1985 p. 371-384.

[7] London J C, Weniger J H. 1996b. Investigation into traditionally managed Djallonké-sheep production in humid and sub humid zones of Asante, Ghana. V. Productivity indices. *J. Anim. Breed. Genet*. 113, 483-492

[8] Pinot R, Teissier J.-H, Bauchau P. l'allaitement artificiel des agneaux. I. - Comparaison entre différents laits de remplacement et le lait de brebis. Annales de zootechnie, INRA/EDP Sciences, 1965, 14 (3), pp.261-278. hal-00886848

[9] Toukourou Y, Abdoulaye M, Attakpa Y E, Alkoiret I T. Croissance des agneaux Djallonkes nourris avec du lait de soja, Tropicultura 2016 vol. 34 no. 2 p. 150-157

[10] Kassa S K, Salifou C F A, Dayo G K, Ahounou G S, Dotché O I, Issifou T M, Houaga I, Kountinhouin G B, Mensah G A, Yapi-Gnaoré V, Youssao A K I. Production de lait des vaches Bororo blanches et Borgou en élevage traditionnel au Bénin. Livestock Research for Rural Development 28 (9) 2016

[11] Toléba S S, Youssao A K I, Dahouda M, Missainhoun U M A, Mensah G A. Identification et valeurs nutritionnelles des aliments utilisés en élevage d'aulacodes (*Thryonomys swinderianus*) dans les villes de Cotonou et Porto-Novo au Bénin. *Bulletin de la Recherche Agronomique du Bénin Numéro 64 – Juin 2009.*

[12] FAO. http://www.fao.org/3/CA2804FR/ca2804fr.pdf

[13] Bokossa I Y, Tchekessi C K C, Dossou-Yovo P, Egounlety M, Dossa R M. Substitution partielle du lait en poudre par le lait de soja pour la production du yaourt. *Bulletin de la Recherche Agronomique du Bénin. Numéro 69 – Juin 2011*

[14] CNUCED. Soja. Un profil de produit de base par INFOCOMM. Fonds de la CNUCED pour l'information sur les marchés des produits de base agricoles. Nations Unies. New York et Genève, 2016. https://unctad.org/fr/PublicationsLibrary/INFOCOMM_cp10_SoyaBeans_fr.pdf

[15] BELABBES M M. Qualité Nutritionnelle et Aptitude de Transformation Technologique du Lait de Brebis selon le Système d'élevage. Faculté des Sciences de la Nature et de la Vie. Thèse de doctorat. 2019

[16] Gbangboché A B, Abiola F A, Laporte J P, Salifou S, Leroy P L. 2002. Amélioration des ovins dans l'Ouémé et le Plateau en République du Bénin: enjeux de croisement des ovins Djallonké avec les moutons du Sahel. ; Tropicultur*a,* **20**, 2, 70-75.

[17] Senou M, Dahouda M C, Adandédjan C, Aboki V, Alimy S, Tondji P M. Pre- and post-weaning growth in Djallonké lambs; Livestock Research for Rural Development 21 (6); Trop. Vet. 4, 2009. p. 67-70